GAVIN LEVY

Acting Games for Individual Performers

A comprehensive
workbook of 110
acting exercises

MERIWETHER PUBLISHING LTD.
Colorado Springs, Colorado

Meriwether Publishing Ltd., Publisher
PO Box 7710
Colorado Springs, CO 80933-7710

Editor: **Theodore O. Zapel**
Associate editor: **Audrey Scheck**
Cover design: **Jan Melvin**

© Copyright MMVII Meriwether Publishing Ltd.
Printed in the United States of America
First Edition

Library of Congress Cataloging-in-Publication Data

Levy, Gavin.
  acting games for individual performers : a comprehensive workbook of 110
  acting exercises / by Gavin Levy.
    p. cm.
  ISBN-13: 978-1-56608-146-7 (pbk.)
  ISBN-10: 1-56608-146-7 (pbk.)
1. Acting. 2. Improvisation (Acting) I. Title.
PN2061.L389 2007
792.02'8--dc22

2007016289

1   2   3   07   08   09

Table of Contents

Acknowledgments

With special thanks to:

Albert, Stella, and Roxanne Levy for all of their support throughout the years; David Deacon and Paul G. Gleason, my friends and mentors; and Leslie Harding for all of her hard work.

Introduction

This book is a collection of exercises that are to be utilized by the individual actor. Whether you lean more towards film or theatre, this book will be of importance to you. It is as beneficial for the beginning student as it is for the seasoned professional. It enables you to explore at your own level and at your own pace. You get to become your own teacher and guide; there is no set order for you to follow. This puts the responsibility squarely on your shoulders. It is your journey and yours alone; you get to decide which direction it needs to take. The material is so versatile that it is beneficial for actors of all levels from individuals to groups.

While I encourage all actors to take workshops on a regular basis, many actors are unable to do so. Working too many hours in their jobs, having insufficient funds, and/or not finding the workshops that appeal to them are a number of reasons. With *Acting Games for Individual Performers*, you are going to be able to continue your journey of self-discovery in your own time and place. The majority of exercises in this book may be done in the comfort of your own home, while others may be completed in a public place of your choice. You do not have to go to an acting studio to work these exercises. You are going to be able to sharpen your tools and enhance your skills on an ongoing basis.

If we accept the premise that, as actors, the only instrument we have is ourselves, then it stands to reason that we should want to explore that instrument — utilize it to its full potential.

This book does not come from a specific theory on acting or profess a definitive technique. Rather, it runs the gamut of grabbing, creating, molding, and inventing any exercise or activity that can be utilized and explored by the actor/student for his/her gain. The purpose of this book is simply to utilize these exercises in moving forward in your work as an actor.

This book is not for everybody; it is for the serious actor/student who is interested in the hard work and dedication it takes to explore the craft of acting. Nobody can experience these moments or make these discoveries for you. It is going to take time and effort to find some of the answers. The good news is that you can do the work at your own pace, working around your own schedule. If you simply sit down and read this book, you are wasting your time and money. This is a "doing" book, and you must be up and moving to fully experience this work.

To each actor that I work with I ask these two questions: Are you looking to put a stamp on your work? Do you care if your work has any value, or is it simply about booking jobs and making money? I am all for an actor booking work and making money, but if the quality of your work has no real meaning, if searching for truth in your acting is the last thing on your mind, if getting your character's viewpoint across to the audience is meaningless to you, then please put this book back on the shelf and save your money. If you want to develop your craft on an ongoing basis, however, open the book and begin to discover, explore, and enjoy the journey, for it is your journey alone.

Games

Each game/exercise is listed under a certain chapter. This is to give you an idea of where you can go to find a certain type of exercise. If you want to work on an improvisation exercise, you can go to the chapter heading that applies to this. If you find an activity in improvisation, it is important to know that the same activity may also fit into other categories such as characterization and research. This is because many of these activities have benefits that will cross over into other areas. Use each chapter heading as a guideline rather than a set rule.

Variables

For most of the games I offer a variable so you can see how the game can be utilized in another way. However, I have not included variables in all the activities. I want you to see if you can come up with your own so that you can continue to utilize your imagination and enhance your creativity. The idea behind this section is to encourage you to come up with as many variables of your own as you can. Too often, actors become a passive part of the process. I want you to use this opportunity to take an active role and make your own discoveries.

Discussion

Each game comes with its own discussion section. These are self-discussion sections for you to break down each game and make further findings on your own. I have often heard actors say, "Tell me what you want me to do and I can do it." While this is indeed an admirable offer, it takes ownership away from the actor. The self-discussion sections will give you the confidence to take each game in any direction you choose while understanding your reasons for doing so. As an actor you want to get to a place where you don't need another person to tell you why you should do something or react in a certain way. You want to be able to solve any challenge that comes up by virtue of your own intelligence. You will also find that when you are given specific direction, you will be able to mold, shape, and bend yourself in any given way because you are able to ask yourself specific questions. Do not become the pawn on the chessboard when you have the opportunity to be the king or queen. Take time out of an exercise to delve into the discussion portion. While it is true that "acting is in the doing," it is equally true that for the doing to have any cohesive value it needs to be explored through the discussion process.

Purpose

There are two purpose sections that accompany each game. I encourage you to come up with as many other purposes as you can. This is important because it lets you know why you are being asked to explore each game. Without a purpose section you may have a lot of fun and a lot of discovery, but you would be left with little understanding of the benefits of the work you are doing. The more you understand why you are doing something, the more far-reaching the benefits.

When you finish this book, it does not mean you've reached the end of the road. This book is a continuation of this wonderful acting path you are on. This book doesn't have a beginning, middle, or end and neither does your acting journey. The aim of this book is not to make every moment of your acting organic or inspired, rather it is to create the full potentiality to allow your acting to be organic and inspired.

Chapter 1
Creative State

1. The Power of Positive Thinking

I am sure you have heard about the power of positive thinking. A lot of us agree that it is important, but we do not integrate it into our lives. As an actor, a positive outlook is an essential part of your journey. For this game, buy a book that is related to positive thinking. A favorite book of mine is *Think and Grow Rich* by Napoleon Hill.

Too often, individuals buy a book only to read the first ten pages. I want you to read your empowering book from cover to cover. Take the advice that you think is valuable and follow through with action. It is all very well to read a book, but if you don't incorporate it into your life, it is not that beneficial.

Go to the library or look through a selection of books at the bookstore before deciding which one to purchase. Once you have completed your book, review the concepts you have gained. You don't have to finish this book in a particular time frame; take as long as you need so that you can start to apply what you are learning at your own pace. Buy another book that relates to positive thinking once you have finished your first one.

Variables:

Find quotes that are related to having a positive outlook on life. Take your favorite ones and make them into a poster to hang on your wall.

Discussion:

What was your opinion on positive thinking before you started this exercise?

Take a moment to think about your life and your outlook on life.

Why is it so important for the actor to have a good attitude?

Purpose:

To incorporate positive thinking with action into your life

It is so important for you, as an actor, to have a positive outlook on life because your profession is full of challenges. Directors enjoy working with actors who are positive and can be a calm influence where chaos is sometimes the order of the day. Actors who have a wonderful outlook on life and bring this energy to their work stick out and are quite often remembered by the director for future projects. If an actor goes to each audition believing that he will not get the role, more than likely he will find himself right. If an actor goes to an audition and does not get the role but knows that she did her best and learns from the experience, she will have a much smoother and more enjoyable journey.

To enjoy your life

We have all heard the phrase, "suffer for your art." While it is true that there is a great deal of sacrifice needed to succeed in the world of acting, it is not a given that you have to suffer. Why be an actor if you are going to spend your life in misery? When we study some of the greatly-loved movie icons such as James Dean and Marilyn Monroe, we can see that they had enormous challenges with self-esteem in their own lives even though they were adored by their public. You may say that it is far-fetched for an actor to actually enjoy his journey, and yet, why not? If you have to work at creating a positive environment, it is much more beneficial than working at creating a negative one. Having a more positive outlook will free your mind to become more creative rather than spending all of your time focused on worry and strife. If you are more creative, you have more potential to grow in your acting and more potential opportunity to work as an actor. Having a positive outlook allows you to create a win-win situation for your life.

2. Chameleon

Start this game first thing in the morning. Take on a persona different from your own and live it fully for one day. Let's say that you are usually a fairly introverted person, and you have chosen "confidence" as your persona. Brush your teeth with confidence, walk down the street with confidence, smile with confidence, breathe with confidence, and order your coffee with confidence. Everything you do today must have the essence of confidence attached. It's not enough to simply appear confident; I want it to permeate at a much deeper level. Tell yourself how confident you are throughout the day: your inner monolog should be completely confidence based. Assert yourself in a confident fashion wherever you go and whatever you do. If you find yourself in a situation where you lack confidence, act as if you have confidence.

As you are going through your day, review what is happening. Make a mental note of any changes that you notice in your own behavior. Perhaps the way you made your peanut butter sandwich, the way you answered the phone, or the way you brushed your hair differed from normal. Keep this going for an entire day and do not stop until you go to bed. You don't need to write anything down for this activity. Instead, you can allow the actual visceral experiences of the day to stay with you.

Another day or week you can take on another persona, perhaps that of a Don Juan who sees himself as absolutely gorgeous. You are not being asked to go out and exaggerate your chosen persona; rather, you are being asked to absorb it. By allowing yourself to be conscious of your newly-chosen trait, you will find it takes on a life of its own. There is no need to force things in an artificial way; be in the moment, wherever that may be. It is a sad fact that sometimes after a performance an actor will say, "I had no idea what I was doing." You should always know what you are doing. You should remain in control of your faculties at all times, otherwise you are simply not acting.

Variables:

Come up with your own.

Discussion:

What was the first thing that you noticed that you did differently today?

How did changing your persona change your physicality?

What was the most profound experience that you had today?

How was this activity beneficial for you?

Purpose:

To stay consistent over a lengthy amount of time

In this game you have to maintain the same persona the entire day. At times you may find that you waver and start to go back to the "old you," and yet you must refocus and rediscover your chosen persona. If you are in a play, you are going to have to sustain your character over a period of time. A number of plays will demand that you stay on-stage for the entire show. If you are not able to sustain your character for this period, it will become inconsistent and contradictory. I am not saying that you should create a one-dimensional character, but rather that you should stay consistent with who you are. If you are playing a well-educated doctor who resides in 1930s-era London and you suddenly start to slouch because you momentarily lost your concentration, you have dispelled in that moment any belief the audience may have had in your character. You have dispelled any belief that you went to a private school or that you were raised with etiquette and impeccable manners. This activity is more simplistic in that you are not delving into the complexities of a complete character, yet staying consistent is a must.

To become accustomed to "doing"

The field of acting is wonderful and fascinating in that it is never ending. I am a firm believer in processing and analyzing your work. I am also a firm believer in the "doing" in acting. In this exercise you are asked to spend an entire day living with a persona that is somewhat foreign to you. You are not being asked to think about it, but to spend your entire day living it. It is through the "doing," not the discussion, that you will experience the effects. In a performance you live with your character and the circumstances in each and every moment. You do not take a break in the middle to come up for air. In this activity I ask you to reflect as you go so that the discoveries become organic. You cannot do this in a performance, for it would contradict the concept of being in the moment. In acting there is a time for analyzing and problem solving (the rehearsal period) and a time for being in the moment (the performance itself). This activity allows you to experience a little bit of both. Uta Hagen correctly says that, "Hopefully, you have understood that whatever is imagined, mentally considered, or thought through should provide stimuli for the body and the soul and the desire to do something about it."[1]

3. Day of Rest

This exercise is as literal as it sounds. Take a day of rest from your normal routines and environment and go do something completely different. Let's say you are used to mailing out your headshots, sending thank you notes and reminders to agents, going to networking engagements, and taking acting classes. Take a total break and go do something as far removed from these things as you can. Perhaps you can spend the day walking in a forest and being with nature. You could go to a lake, have a picnic, and read a book (not on acting). You could go bowling with a group of friends who have no interest in acting. Consider doing something you have never done before. Perhaps you could go bungee jumping or skydiving. Whatever you do, spend the whole day

[1]Uta Hagen, *Respect for Acting* (New York: Macmillan Publishing Company, 1973), 286.

breaking away from the acting world and all that it entails. I want to reiterate that you are to do absolutely no work whatsoever on this day. What I am asking you to do is based on the idea that a change is as good as a rest. Actors often find that once they complete this exercise they feel refreshed and ready to move forward with a newfound energy.

Variables:

Instead of taking a day of rest, try living your day in a different order. If you would normally go to the gym at night, perhaps you could go in the morning instead. Have dinner for breakfast and vice versa. Flip your day completely on its head.

Discussion:

What were your criteria for making sure that you had a total day of rest?

What surprised you most about this day?

Did you find you were able to get more done the following day than you normally would have?

Would you recommend this activity to other friends involved in the acting world? How are you going to sell them on its benefits?

Purpose:

To recharge your batteries

If you are trying to "make it" as a professional actor, then you know that your life can be very demanding. A lot of actors will keep going until they simply burn out. I have worked with a number of actors on the concept that it is important to take time out for themselves and do something completely different. As an actor, you are going to have to be completely self motivated, and at times this will be very tough. By taking a break from the norm, you will be able to recharge and come back with a newfound zest. This is not supposed to be a one-off activity, but one that you can utilize again and again.

To create balance in your life

This may sound the same as recharging, but there is a vital difference. Putting balance in your life is going to help you put everything into perspective. I always talk with actors about enjoying the journey because if you are not enjoying it, it's going to come to an abrupt end. Putting balance into your life will allow your acting to have a fresh spin instead of becoming stale and constrained. When you are constantly feeling stressed and overworked, how are you going to allow your creative juices to flow? It is important to understand that health and balance go side by side. Deepak Chopra observes, "Perfect health, pure and invincible, is a state we have lost. Regain it, and we regain the world."[2] By taking time off every now and then, the task of following your acting dreams will feel a little bit easier and smoother.

4. Creative State

This is a very well-known game that I have chosen to give a different name. For this exercise you'll need a little notebook and a pen or pencil. When you wake up in the morning, take two minutes to write and write and write. Do this within the first thirty minutes of your day. Don't think about what you are writing — just write without stopping. Even if what you are writing doesn't make any sense, keep writing for the full two minutes. Don't wait for something good to come to you; just keep on writing. Once you are finished, you may review what you wrote, but this is not required. Make sure you have a notebook that is set aside for this exercise alone. Find a place of relative quiet before beginning this exercise. This is an exercise to do on a daily basis, so get into the habit. Someone once said, "If your life is worth living, it is worth recording."

Variables:

You could vary the length and write for five minutes or more. You could also experiment by writing at night before going to bed.

Discussion:

How much discipline is required to do this activity on a daily basis?

Were you actually aware of what you were writing as you were writing it?

Use descriptive adjectives to describe the way you feel after completing this exercise each day.

In what way is this exercise playing a significant role in your life?

Purpose:

To find a creative state

This game asks you to write without editing your words. It asks you

---

[2]Deepak Chopra, *Journey into Healing* (New York: Crown Publishers, 1994), 11.

to unleash whatever comes out on paper without censoring it. It is detoxification for the mind. In a way we can say it is unloading whatever is on the mind, even when you didn't know what was on your mind in the first place. By unleashing these words, you are stimulating and cleansing your mind. You are putting your mind in a creative state. This is an excellent way for you as an actor to start your day. If you wake up and the first thing you are thinking about is paying bills or getting your essay assignment complete, these concerns, while valid, will be pulling you away from a creative state. I'm not saying that you should ignore them; I'm saying attend to them after this exercise. It is crucial to be in a creative state when you are working as an actor; it guides you in finding more ways to create work for yourself. All actors have been in a creative state at some point. The question is, for how long? Activities such as this encourage you to live in that creative state.

To create discipline in your work

In this game you must continue on a daily basis. If I asked you to work it one time, that would be easy, but to do so on a daily basis requires discipline. To continue to work this exercise, even when you have other things that need to be done, requires discipline and commitment on your part. The field of acting is similar. No one is going to simply hand you an acting career, so you are going to have to be disciplined. It is up to you to check for auditions, to find an agent, to work your craft, to stay focused, to network, to stay positive and open even when those around you are not, to send out your headshots and resumés, to send out thank you cards, to work your other job, and to stay focused even when things seem to be going nowhere. Know that discipline is going to be your best friend as you continue your acting journey.

5. Reflective Reflections

For this game, stand in front of a mirror and stare at your own reflection for fifteen minutes. As you are doing this, come up with as many reasons as possible why the person staring back at you is an actor/actress. Some possible examples are: "I'm talented," "I work hard," "I'm passionate about acting," "I have a lot of self motivation," "I have a desire to grow and learn," "I have a thick skin," and "There is nothing else I want to do with my life." You do not have to say these out loud, but come up with as many reasons as you can. If after three minutes of looking at your reflection you have come up with all the reasons as to why you should be an actor, keep looking. Spend the entire fifteen minutes reflecting (no pun intended) on why you should act. Even if acting is just a hobby for you, do this exercise. Please do not include any reasons why you should not be an actor, as this is not part of the exercise. After fifteen minutes, write down all of the reasons why you are an actor. Take that piece of paper and stick it somewhere where you will see it on a daily basis.

Variables:

Spend fifteen minutes staring at your reflection and come up with as many answers as you can why the person facing you should be thankful. "I have good friends," "I have freedom to make my own choices," "I have a supportive family," "I have a good education," and so on.

Discussion:

Did you come up with any answers that you had not thought of before?

What was your first impression of your reflection?

Do you buy into the answers you came up with?

What is the benefit of putting this list in a place where you can see it on a daily basis?

Purpose:

To be your own biggest fan

There are so many people willing to tell you why you will not succeed in acting, why you cannot act; there is no need for you to be one of them. By becoming your own biggest fan you are able to encourage yourself while supporting and recognizing the need for constant and never-ending improvement. If you live in a small town, you may find that your teachers, friends, family, and community are very supportive of your acting — when it is not a career, that is. Let's say that at some point you move to London, New York, or Los Angeles to pursue your dreams, and you find that your whole support network has been pulled out from under you. You also find that not only are these cities tough, but everyone there seems to be pursuing the same dreams that you are. As Russell Grandstaff points out, "To be a good actor you almost must have the stamina of a mountain climber, the endurance of a marathon runner, the patience of a turtle, the strength of a weightlifter, the courage of a lion trainer, the memory of a computer, the agility of a gymnast, and the imagination of a child."[3] In other words, there is nothing easy about being or becoming an actor. At this point, it is imperative that you become your own biggest fan. If you do not believe in yourself, who will?

To appreciate the power of repetition
By keeping your list in a prominent place, you will see it every day. By viewing the reasons why you are an actor each and every day, you are utilizing the power of repetition. When we repeat something again and again, our minds look for ways to make these things reality. Let's say that one of the things on your list is, "I'm passionate about acting." If you get to see this every day, you will continue to search for ways to allow this to be a self-fulfilling prophecy. It sounds like a way of tricking the mind, and in a way it is. But anything that benefits you in your acting journey and causes no harm to others should be taken advantage of. "No" is a word you are going to hear a lot throughout your acting career. The repetition of this word over many years can have quite a powerful effect on an actor's life. Allow the word "no" to become a best friend that you can embrace, and move on.

6. Coordination Station

For this exercise, I want you to experience one or all of the following modalities: T'ai Chi, Yoga, Feldenkrais, Alexander Technique, and/or dance (such as ballet, jazz, or tap). Choose whichever one you are most interested in and sign up for some classes. If you take classes in T'ai Chi and find that it is not for you, then take some Alexander classes instead. Sign up for a minimum of four classes so that you have a good idea of what it is all about. There is no reason why you cannot sample or study classes in all of these fields over a period of time. It is also possible to find videos with instruction in all of these areas, but I would like you to experience the work with an instructor. This book is not a substitute to working as an actor or training with an instructor, but rather to complement these areas.

Variables:
Come up with your own.

[3]Russell Grandstaff, *Acting and Directing* (Lincolnwood, IL: National Textbook Company, 1970), 1.

Discussion:

Were you surprised at your findings in your discipline of choice?

What is the most valuable lesson you have learned from this discipline so far?

How would you personally link this field to acting? In your opinion, is there any link to acting?

Purpose:

To develop coordination

In whichever discipline you are working, you are learning about coordination: coordination in movement, body alignment, body awareness, and mobility. One of the most fundamental principles for the actor is coordination. If an actor does not know how to put one foot in front of the other, he is going to be at a disadvantage. You might say this is a totally preposterous assumption, but when an actor is being watched by an audience, all kinds of illogical movements have potential to occur. If you want proof, ask a fellow actor to walk across the room while you stare at her. You are going to see that her walk becomes forced or somewhat too perfect. An actor who is well coordinated can surpass this.

Actors need to be coordinated in voice as well. Suppose you kept gasping for air because of nerves, and you had no control over your vocal instrument. This would send a message of weakness and might contradict your character. Few actors are born with coordination, so you must learn to become coordinated. The question then arises: does an actor have to be coordinated to become a great actor? The answer is no. There are amazing actors who slur their speech and others who walk in a disjointed manner. You might then ask, "Do I need to take yoga to become a better actor?" The answer to this question again is a resounding no; however, it may help your coordination in a big way. Understand that in the world of acting there are no absolutes. Coordination is merely one of the major foundations for the actor's work.

To develop body awareness

In this exercise you learn more about your body and how it works. You have heard time and time again that your body is your only instrument as an actor, and you have to learn how to use it. Imagine that you bought an electric guitar and decided instead of learning how to play you were just going to wing it. Your parents have a lot of money, so they book a club for your first gig and invite all of your friends. You have never played before, but your friends say you look really good when you hold a guitar and that you should be a rock star. You play your first gig and bomb, and you get really upset and don't understand what went wrong. Unfortunately, this is true for many people who call themselves actors. Acting is a craft that takes time, effort, training, exploration, commitment, and performance.

Chapter 2
Imagination

7. In a Word

Choose a word that you will act out in a pantomime style without the use of your voice. Some examples of words are "America," "statue," "greed," "poverty," "freedom," or "adolescence." Your task is not to simply define your word in a literal sense but to explore its wider meaning. For example, if you were going to explore the word "America," you might create a scene of someone rushing to get dressed, rushing to eat breakfast, rushing to get in the car, rushing to get to work, rushing to get into the office, and finally making it to the office and putting his feet up on the desk and twiddling his thumbs in boredom. This activity appears to be a simple one, yet to define the greater meaning of your chosen word is a complex task. There is no time limit to your scene, if it lasts twenty minutes then so be it.

Once you have worked with one word, come back to this activity another time and choose a different word. If you are stuck for a word choice, use your dictionary or ask friends for words that have profound meaning to them.

Variables:

Instead of using a word, use a sound. Perhaps you could base your scene on a beating drum, a clashing symbol, or a ringing bell. Listen to the sound before commencing. This will give you a real kinesthetic sense of the deeper meaning of your sound.

Discussion:

Why did you choose that particular word to interpret?

Did your scene really explore your chosen word in its entirety?

If you had an audience, would you be tempted to make the scene more entertaining?

Why did you choose to interpret the word in that way? Make sure you can justify your answer.

Purpose:

**To find the deeper meaning to the words
given to us by the playwright**

What is it that the playwright wants to say? What are the messages she is attempting to get across? I like to give the actor this exercise because it can make a far-reaching point. If one word can have so much meaning, so much depth, and so much to say, then it becomes impossible to look at a script without attempting to find the deeper meaning behind the words. As Hamlet once said, "Speak the speech, I pray you, as I pronounced it to you, trippingly on the tongue."[1] If you don't know the meaning of a word or understand its background, how are you going to be able to interpret the way a word needs to be used? This activity plants a seed suggesting that words are not just words but have a far deeper meaning when explored fully.

To comprehend that words have different meanings to different people

If you took the word "freedom" and had two people interpret it in a scene, you would end up with two totally different scenes. One person might interpret "freedom" by recreating a scene from a slave ship, breaking free from shackles, jumping off the boat, drowning, and finally being free. Another person might create a scene of a rich woman driving a beautiful Mercedes Benz while stroking her chinchilla fur and sipping chilled champagne. Both scenes are totally legitimate and yet vastly different interpretations of the word "freedom." It is important to realize that our interpretation of the words on the page is constrained only by the limitations we put upon them.

8. Truisms

This is one of those exercises that will probably make you ask, "What does this have to do with acting?" Once you complete the activity, I think you will have a clear picture.

Come up with a list of truisms. Examples would be: "Everyone has had the experience of nodding his head 'yes' or shaking it 'no' even without quite realizing it;" "You already know how to experience pleasant sensations;" and "Each of us was born into the world." A truism is not necessarily universal — for instance, a quadriplegic may not have the experience of being able to nod his head — but it should be as close to universal as you can get. See if you can come up with your own list of ten truisms. Review your list (it should be written down) to make sure that your truisms are truly universal. "Everyone likes ice cream," for example, is an incorrect statement. Take time to make sure your list is as accurate as possible.

Variables:

[1]William Shakespeare, *The Complete Works of William Shakespeare* (London: Abbey Library, 1978), 863.

Memorize your truisms; you are not allowed to write them down. This is a more challenging task. I am not asking you to vaguely remember your truisms; I want you to remember them with very specific detail. Give yourself a time limit in which to complete the task. If you want to make it even more challenging, then any time you make a mistake (such as coming up with a false truism) start your list entirely from scratch.

Discussion

What is the purpose of this activity?

At any point did you go back and change your answers? What was your reason for doing so?

How long did this activity take you?

Was there any point when you felt like giving up? What made you give up or allowed you to keep going?

Purpose

To problem solve and conquer challenges

In this activity you have to problem solve to come up with your truism. You might come up with an answer and then realize that your statement is incorrect. Now you will have to go back and start again. Let's say that you have been on one hundred auditions and not booked a single one. This could be an extreme run of bad luck, or maybe you need to sit down and problem solve. Are you prepared for each audition? How do you act when you enter the room? Do you have good listening skills and take direction well? Is your agent sending you out for the right types of auditions? To become a successful working actor you have to understand the art of problem solving and apply it on a regular basis.

To use your brain

This exercise requires a lot of thinking. Many people are under the impression that actors lead a glamorous life. An actor should actually engage in a studious life. There is so much to learn in the field of acting. If you studied continuously for the rest of your life, you would still have plenty left to discover. How much do you know about the history of acting? How much do you read about acting? How many movies do you watch and critique at the same time? This exercise will remind you to be constantly using your brain. The mind is so powerful, and its benefits to the actor are limitless. Deepak Chopra explores the idea that, "We are the only creatures on earth who can change our biology by what we think and feel."[2] This is profound information for the actor and should increase your desire to utilize your brain to its full potential.

9. Walk the Line

Find an open space and picture an imaginary line that goes from one end of the space to the other. Walk along the imaginary line in a comfortable fashion. When you are finished, note how you feel as you prepare to go again. This time, imagine that your line is a tightrope that is four feet in the air. With this information, use caution to walk along the rope. When you are finished, note what you did differently from the first time. Take a moment to walk around the room and regain your composure. When you come back, imagine that your rope is now thirty feet in the air. Walk along the rope with the knowledge that if you fall, you will drop thirty feet. As you proceed, do so with honesty and commitment. When you are finished, pay attention to what has just been going on in your body and see if you notice any differences from the previous two occasions. Take a few minutes to walk around and regain your composure. This is the fourth and final time you will be asked to walk along the rope. It is going to be the most challenging of all. This time, imagine your rope is two hundred feet above the Grand Canyon. There are razor-sharp shards of rock soaring skyward in your direction. If you fall, you will certainly meet a grisly death. An enormous fire is roaring behind you, and you have only three minutes to make it across the rope before the flames engulf you. You are the sole breadwinner for your family, and if you die, your family will lose their home and all of their possessions. Before you begin, prepare yourself in a way befitting this task. When you commence, remember the enormously high stakes and that there are time constraints to bear in mind. Once you are finished, review how you coped in this section and what was going through your mind.

It is possible that you could fall at any stage in any section of this exercise. If you fell in the first or second parts of this activity, the consequences would be fairly minor. If you fell in the third or fourth stages, the results would be quite severe. Once you have finished the entire exercise, let everything sink in. Have you just conquered the Grand Canyon or met your doom trying?

[2]Deepak Chopra, *Journey into Healing* (New York: Crown Publishers, 1994), 28.

Variables:

Come up with your own.

Discussion:

How important was it for you to succeed in the first part of this exercise?

How did the importance shift when your life was on the line?

How did you feel physically different from the first time to the fourth time?

What changed when there was a specific time element added?

Purpose:

To commit to your objectives

The further you go in this exercise, the more important it becomes to commit to your objectives. As the stakes become higher, the need to succeed is intensified. As an actor, you want to commit to your character's objectives at every turn. Objectives do not always have to be complex or clever; however, they do need to be executed by the actor. Let's say you are playing a judge in a court scene. Your objective might be to wrap the case up because you have had a long day and you want to go home and put your feet up. This may be the overall objective, and within the scene you may have mini-objectives such as putting the prosecutor in his place because he is being rude. Be sure that your objectives have a purpose. If you said, "My objective is to play the judge," this is not an actual objective. If you have no clear objectives, your work will become clouded, gray, and muddled.

To utilize your imagination

In this exercise you are always on the ground, and yet through your imagination you end up two hundred feet above the Grand Canyon on a rope engulfed in flames. This activity requires a rather creative imagination to create a sense of realism. Time and time again in your acting you are going to have to use your imagination to create truths. Let's say you are on a studio floor that is supposedly a beautiful beach. The floor is hard, lights are shining in your face, camera operators, assistant directors, and producers are all running around in the background, and you have to create the appearance of being on a beautiful, secluded beach. It is going to take all of your powers of concentration and imagination for you to believe this scenario, but if you do not believe it, how can you expect your audience to do so? Look for opportunities throughout your day to work with and explore your imagination.

10. Channeling

Take a seat in a comfortable chair. Put your right hand on your lap and bring your thumb and fourth finger together so that they are almost touching. I will explain the reason for this in a moment. Think of a specific memory of a time when you were incredibly relaxed. Let's assume for the moment that your memory is of lying on the beach sometime last year. With your eyes closed, picture that experience. Take your picture and make it brighter. Now, take your picture and turn it into a moving picture like a short film. Imagine yourself lying on the beach, content and relaxed. Imagine the sounds of the waves as they gently crash against the shore. Perhaps you can hear the sound of the seagulls flying above. Now make the picture even bigger and more intense. The clearer the picture becomes, the more deeply you go into relaxation. Allow yourself to smell the salt water and feel the gentle spray of the waves as you go even deeper into relaxation. When you feel you are at the height of relaxation, bring your fourth finger and thumb together and keep them together for the next five to ten seconds. It is imperative that you do not bring them together until you are at the height of relaxation. Keep your eyes closed, as you are still visualizing at this point. When you are finished, relax your hand and open your eyes. Take a moment to bring your body back to balance. Walk around for a little bit and shake your body out. Now, bring your fourth finger and thumb back together. If this has worked correctly, you should feel a slight feeling of relaxation going through your entire body.

What we have just done is channeled the feeling of relaxation through your thumb and finger. Through this exercise, any time in the future that you bring your thumb and fourth finger of your right hand together, you will experience a slight feeling of relaxation. The exciting part of this activity is that you still have another seven fingers to work with. In your own time, channel different positive emotions through your other fingers. These could be anything: laughter, creativity, confidence, love, etc. It is very important that you use a different finger for each emotion and that you remember which emotion went with which finger. An easy way to do this is to draw your two hands and label each finger with the chosen emotion. If you find that once you have channeled your emotion it does not have the desired effect, go back and repeat the exercise. Only if you bring your thumb and finger together at the moment when the emotion is at its peak will you truly be able to channel it. If you do this again and it still does not work, come up with a different memory. There is no rush to complete this task. Take it slow; channel one finger a week if you like.

Variables:

Come up with your own.

Discussion:

Were you able to pick specific stories from your past to guide you in this exercise?

How is this channeling exercise beneficial and complementary to your acting?

What happened in terms of intensity as you added sound, brighter lights, smells, and a moving picture?

At any point did you feel like giving up on this activity? What kept you going?

Purpose:

To explore your acting in an experimental fashion

Imagine you are in the middle of a scene where the character you are playing suddenly has a boost of confidence. It might be interesting at that precise moment to channel your confidence finger. Perhaps it would give you a momentary boost of impulsive confidence and impulsive behavior. Acting is full of possibilities by trial and error and discovery. There is so much more to discover in the craft of acting, and there are many questions left unanswered. As an esteemed colleague of mine once commented, "It is not 'what is the answer?' but rather, 'what is the question?'"

To benefit your day-to-day life

This exercise asks you to channel positive emotions into your body and mind. Any day you choose, you will be able to get that little boost of confidence or relaxation or joy. It is not all encompassing, but rather a gentle reminder of some of the beneficial emotions to incorporate into your life. An actor's life can be stressful because it involves rejection and uncertainty about income and employment. This exercise serves as a small way to redress that balance. The more ways you can find to make your journey an enjoyable one, the more ways you will have to create longevity in your career.

11. Imagination Station

This is a fairly well-known exercise that I think you will enjoy. I am going to give you the delightful opportunity to discover your imagination. Close your eyes, hold your arms out in front of you and imagine you have a bucket in one hand and 100 helium-filled balloons in the other. Now imagine that water is beginning to fill the bucket. Use your imagination to see and hear the water pouring in. Perhaps you feel the water as it splashes gently against your skin. Feel the bucket getting heavier and heavier. Now discover that you have an ever-increasing number of helium balloons. See them, hear them gently bumping into one another, and feel them as they slowly begin to pull your hand up, up, and up. Now, notice that the bucket is getting fuller and heavier and someone has recently added a heavy weight to your bucket. You realize that you arm is getting heavier and heavier and there is a sensation of pulling on your hand. Now, bring you attention back to your hand with the balloons. Perhaps it feels lighter and lighter as the number of balloons steadily increases. When you are ready, keep your arms where they are and open your eyes. Notice how much your arms have moved since the beginning of the exercise. Do you see that imagination is the language of the subconscious? The mind thinks in pictures and images. As an actor, it is important to have some understanding of how your mind works. When you are finished, review your findings for this activity.

Variables:

Change the objects you are holding; perhaps you have a heavy weight in one hand and a hot air balloon in the other.

Discussion:

Did you find that your arms had moved? Were you surprised to the extent that this happened?

Is it beneficial for an actor to have an understanding of the language of the subconscious? Explore your answer fully.

Purpose:

To experience firsthand the imagination's effect on the subconscious

In this exercise you are most likely going to find that one arm has raised and the other arm has lowered. It is interesting to note that at no time were you asked to raise or lower your arms, and yet this is precisely what happened. By utilizing your imagination you have caused a physical response in your body. You have influenced your subconscious by exploring your imagination. The subconscious is a powerful part of human nature and has an influence on pretty much everything we do. The imagination is the ally of the actor and can take your acting to an entirely new realm. In his book, *Giant Steps*, Anthony Robbins quotes Einstein as saying, "Imagination is more powerful than knowledge."[3] In this exercise you get to experience firsthand the power of your imagination. Oftentimes you will not be on location, but on a studio set or a theatre stage or in front of a green screen. You are going to need all the imagination you can muster to convince us that you are in a castle instead of a studio stage. As you are looking for justifications as to why you should utilize the exercises in this book, it is very important that you connect them to the bigger picture of your acting career.

To raise the question of the process of acting

There are so many different schools of thought on what acting is and how to do it best. There are so many different techniques that an actor can become confused and disoriented in the process. You have to take this journey on your own because it is yours and no one else can live it for you. This exercise raises the importance of the imagination and highlights ways in which it can influence your actions and feelings. I'm not telling you that you must use your imagination; only you can decide on its value. This is the beauty of your acting journey: while people can suggest that you study this, use that, and explore the other, in the end only you can decide what is right and what truly works for you. Laurence Olivier did not believe in internalizing his acting in any way, and yet he is arguably one of the greatest actors that ever lived. If asked what his secret was, he would most likely say that he did what worked best for him. Find out what works in your acting and then find more.

[3] Anthony Robbins, *Giant Steps* (New York: Simon and Schuster, 1994), 96.

12. Acting Is Everywhere

This exercise was lent to me by my good friend and acting instructor/director, Paul Gleason. Pick up any book in the world, provided it is in a language you can read. Then turn to any page in the book and put your finger on any word. Starting from this word, read the next two sentences out loud. Let these two sentences sink in for a moment. Next, take the sentences and relate them in some way to the world of acting. For example, let's say your sentences read, "On Tuesdays I like to go out and buy milk, which I have with my cookies. I always find it soothing to have a glass of milk and cookies." I know what you are thinking, "How in the world can I relate this sentence to acting?" Let's look at it together. In the first sentence, the individual talks about the fact that he buys cookies and milk every Tuesday. This tells us that human beings can be creatures of habit. It tells us something about human nature, which is very important for the actor in terms of character development. Let's look at the second sentence now and see what we can come up with. The individual tells us that he finds milk and cookies to be soothing. This tells us that food and drink have the potential to affect our nervous system. That is pretty powerful information for the actor to have. If certain foods have the potential to change or influence the way we think and feel, should we not take into account what we are eating before an audition or a performance? You might come up with totally different links to acting than the ones I just mentioned. I am not saying this is going to be an easy exercise; in fact it is going to be quite a challenge. But there is nothing wrong with challenging yourself as an actor. Remember that you can pick up any book to do this exercise.

Variables:

Take any two sentences you hear on television or in a movie and proceed in the same fashion.

Discussion:

Did you select a book randomly?

What was the biggest challenge you found with linking these sentences to acting?

Do you believe there is a sentence that cannot in any way be linked to the field of acting? Justify your answer.

What is acting?

Purpose:

To constantly be thinking about acting

I met a man one time who was passionate about science. His life was science, and he told me that science was everywhere. He could relate any situation to science. In this exercise you are asked to take random information and link it to acting in some way. It may take some practice, and it may come easier as your knowledge in the field of acting grows. The aim of this activity is to get you thinking about acting on a regular basis. Once you see that everything can be linked to acting, you will start to look at the world around you differently. If acting is constantly on your brain, you will be more likely to make discoveries and observations that you might have missed otherwise. This exercise is encouraging you to use your resources for your acting, and the world around you is full of resources.

To make organic connections in your acting

The more connections you make to acting, the more your thought processes will be in tune with the world of acting. The process will become organic for you so that you begin to automatically think in this manner. As an actor, you will sometimes feel clumsy and awkward as if you do not quite fit in your skin. The harder you work and the more you dedicate yourself to the craft, the more organic acting will become for you. You will always work at your craft, but your acting will begin to appear effortless to an audience as you become more in tune with your instrument. To be organic means your acting becomes whole, natural, healthy, pure, and alive.

13. Dentist Delights

This is an exercise that you should do when you are at the dentist. Wait until you are going for something that is going to have a fairly high degree of sensitivity, such as a root canal, a tooth being pulled, a cavity being filled, or something equally fun. As soon as the procedure starts, close your eyes and transport yourself to the beach. Imagine yourself lying on the beautiful golden sand with sun rays glowing across your skin and giving you that warm tingling sensation that allows you to relax deeper and deeper. You may feel the dentist drill, use a syringe, or have other interesting things happening inside your mouth, but even so, bring your focus back to lying on the beach. Feel the spray of the waves as they brush across your skin. Listen to the sound of the seagulls above.

Of course, the dentist may ask you questions. If this happens, answer the dentist and then transport yourself back to the beach. As you lie on the sand, think about the fact that there is nowhere else you need to be and nothing else you need to do. See if you can allow your breathing to slow down and release. Let everything go as you lie on the sand with nothing else to think about except enjoying this wonderful time on the beach. Every now and then you may find yourself drawn back to what is happening in the dentist's chair. Become aware of what is going on inside your body and make a mental note. You may be surprised to find you have not been paying particular attention to the procedure. Each time you check in, take a few moments and then transport yourself back to the beach. Once the dentist tells you that everything is complete, take a few moments to review how much you were present during the procedure and how much time you were able to spend transporting yourself to the beach.

Variables:

You could work in the same way when you are having some form of procedure in the hospital or an injection at the doctor's office.

Discussion:

What was the most pleasant aspect of this exercise?

Were there any physiological changes that you were aware of while lying on the beach?

Do you think this exercise allowed the intensity of being at the dentist to become a more pleasant experience?

In what ways does this exercise contradict the reality in which you find yourself?

Purpose:

To work within contradictions

If you have ever had some sort of surgery at the dentist's office, you know that it is not a particularly enjoyable experience. If you are able to transport yourself to the beach while a drill is in your mouth, this is pretty empowering. It shows that you are developing a great deal of understanding of how to use your imagination. This behavior is also quite contradictory because while in theory you should be experiencing discomfort, instead you are focusing your efforts on having a wonderful time at the beach. In your acting you are going to find yourself in contradictory situations all the time. Perhaps you are in a play where you are supposed to be in a solitary prison cell. This is the reality of the play, and yet there are six hundred people in the audience watching your performance. The reality of the environment is therefore contradictory of the reality of the performance. Perhaps you are playing a scene in a movie where you are breaking up with your boyfriend. The scene itself is very intimate and personal. In reality, there are cameramen, the director, assistant director, lighting technicians, makeup artists, background actors, and a whole array of other people on the set. As an actor, it is necessary to transport yourself to wherever you need to be no matter what reality surrounds you.

To highlight our ability to influence physical and chemical changes within the body

As you are lying in the dentist's office wouldn't it be fascinating if you could release endorphins into your body? As you imagine you are lying on the beach, this may be the reality of what is happening inside your body. As you are receiving an injection into the side of your inner cheek, you are lying on the beach releasing endorphins. This is a profound experience for an actor. I want to continue to raise the idea of how, as an actor, you can influence the chemical releases in your body. As has been said time and time again, acting is a subjective art. By raising questions, I am opening the way for you to come up with the answers. In an art such as acting there are not so many concrete and definitive answers as there are possibilities. One actor might walk a different road from another, and yet the results can be just as beautiful. Laurence Olivier and Constantin Stanislavski had totally different approaches to acting, and yet both left their mark on history. Who is to say what is correct or incorrect? Who is to say what is right or wrong?

Chapter 3
Observation

14. Animal Magic

Begin this exercise by observing an animal of your choice. Perhaps you have a dog or cat you can observe, or maybe your neighbor has a dog. If you choose a more exotic animal, then go visit your local zoo or watch a wildlife documentary. Spend a good week observing your animal without imitating it in any way. You may choose to make notes, but allow what you see to sink in before acting upon it.

After about a week, start imitating your animal in every way you can think of. Imitate its movements, its mannerisms, its sounds, its walk, its eating habits, and its play habits. You are not performing this for anyone but yourself, so throw caution to the wind.

This is not a one-session exploration. Go back to this activity over a period of days — or weeks if need be — until you feel fully satisfied that you have taken on the characteristics of your animal. Explore your animal in different situations. How does it act when it is hungry, concerned, or in fear? Discover the very essence of your animal.

Variables:

Emulate an insect of your choice. This will be a more advanced exercise because your attention to detail will need to be very specific.

Discussion:

What were the benefits of imitating an animal?

Why did you choose that specific animal to imitate? Did you opt for an animal that you thought would be easy to imitate? Were you correct in your assumptions?

If you found you could not let go during this activity, why do you think that was the case?

At what point do you think you went from being you to becoming your animal?

How much time were you prepared to put into this activity? Was it enough?

Purpose:

To develop your observational skills

Too often actors make assumptions about a scene or a character without taking the time to let the true characteristics sink in. In this exercise you are asked to observe, observe, and go back and observe some more. Each time you go back, you may make new discoveries. Each time you watch your animal, you may find that it adds a new element to its movement that you had not noticed before. If you approach your character in a scene and make immediate assumptions without giving yourself time for new findings and discoveries, then you may find yourself with a limited and one-dimensional character. Take the time to observe, discover, observe, and discover some more.

To lose your inhibitions

When an actor says, "I am saving it for the performance," the subtext could be, "I'm not ready to let go yet; I don't feel comfortable in my character's shoes." Part of the aim of this activity is to let go in a big way. The beauty of imitating an animal is that you can't "kind of" let go; you either commit to the animal or you don't. Stella Adler says, "The purpose of the animal exercises is to rid the actor of his social mask and to free him of his inhibitions."[1] Oftentimes animal movements are so extreme or different from our own that there is no time for inhibitions. You may find yourself rolling around on the floor or attempting to scratch the back of your ear with your left foot. In fact, you are giving yourself a whole new set of references that will serve as a starting point for future work. Holding back and waiting for the performance may be your preference, but the more you hold back in the rehearsal process the less opportunity you will have to discover where you can really go with the scene. By letting go, you can live in discovery instead of trying to find it.

15. Movie Critic

Rent two movies. One of the movies should be either an Oscar winner that you have seen before or a movie that you think is amazing. The other movie should be something that looks absolutely awful or that you know is a dreadful movie.

When you get home, start to watch the really bad movie. I am not going to torture you and make you watch the whole thing, but when you get to a part that is unbearably bad, pause the movie. Now look at what is happening on the screen and make some assumptions about why the scene is so bad. For instance, there may be no eye contact between the

---

[1]Stella Adler, *The Technique of Acting* (New York: Bantam Books, 1988), 16.

actors, an actor may be smiling an obviously fake smile, the setting may be very fake looking, one character may be shaking his fist in apparent anger and yet his fist appears to be loose and weak. Go on in this manner and find as many flaws as you can. Do this with several different scenes in the movie. Instead of freezing the film, you may have a scene play in slow motion.

Once you have had your fill of that movie, move onto the great movie. This has to be a movie that literally blows you away. Follow the same procedure as before, only this time find scenes that you feel are absolutely outstanding, freeze them, and note what stands out. For example, you can see the intensity in an actor's eyes, the energy is literally coming out of his fingers, his body appears loose and limp like a dead corpse, her lips are pursed in frustration. Compare your notes from the two movies. You can use this exercise again and again. Any time you rent a movie and feel the urge to do so, pause it, make your observations, and enjoy (or not) the rest of the movie.

Variables:

Watch the same two movies, only this time close your eyes and listen to the dialog. When you get to a place of interest, pause the video and write down what you notice. You may notice things like a shaking voice, forced inflection, stilted timing, heavy breathing, etc. Hopefully for the movie you love, you will find that you have many positive comments. Look at your findings from the two movies and decide what your discoveries mean to you as an actor.

For another variable, see Exercise 97: Movie Critique (page 200).

Discussion:

What were your criteria for choosing the bad movie and the good movie?

How did pausing the movie give you a different method of analyzing the acting?

How can stillness indicate action?

Is pausing the movie a help or a hindrance? Explain your answer.

Purpose:

To create a litmus test for the performance

If you have watched any major sporting event, you will know that the referees are often booed for making bad decisions. The television commentators are able to watch the action on the replay and make some very clear observations. The poor referee, on the other hand, has to make split-second decisions and take the flack if he happens to make a mistake. In this exercise you are given the benefit of technology to pause the action and break it down into minute amounts of detail. If your opinion was that this was an incredible scene, then the hypothesis might be that when you pause it you will find some of the reasons as to why that is. We have the benefit of technology that was not available until fairly recently, so take advantage of it to help your acting.

To develop your sense of sight

You have to be a keen observer to pick up on everything that the still frame gives you. You need to look closely to make sure you didn't miss anything. Someone should write a book called *Observation and the Actor*, for actors always need to be observing what is happening in their environment. This activity allows you to exercise your sense of sight and make attention to detail an automatic process. When an individual first learns to drive a car, he is not particularly good and it takes time, focus, and effort to improve. After a certain period of time, driving becomes an automatic process for most people. Eventually, if you utilize these activities enough you will automatically use your senses at a heightened level of awareness. Richard Boleslavsky comments on the senses when he says, "Learn how to govern this scale, how with your entire being to concentrate on your senses, to make them work artificially, to give them different problems and create the solutions."[2] Without the use of your senses, your performance will always be lost in a falsehood instead of in the land of possibilities.

16. Life Stages

This is not so much an exercise as a lifestyle adaptation. Whenever you are present at a profound event, make mental notes on everything you observe. Let's say you are walking down the street and you see a tow truck about to tow a car, and at the same moment the owner comes back demanding that his car be released. This is a heightened situation; instead of just walking by, make a mental record of all you see. What was the physical condition of the car owner — did his body get tense? Did the veins in his neck start to show? Did he start to shout, or did he

---

[2]Richard Boleslavsky, *Acting* (New York: Theatre Arts Books, 1990), 24.

stay calm? Did the tow truck driver release the car? How was he reacting in comparison with the car's owner? You may not want to get too close to the action, so you may view subtly from the other side of the street. Before you move on, allow the information to sink in.

There are heightened moments happening all around you, so become accustomed to utilizing and learning from these situations. Actors are constantly asked to portray and understand why people do the things they do, and experiencing this firsthand gives you a wonderful toolbox.

A heightened situation does not have to be a tense moment. Perhaps you witness someone scratching a lottery ticket, or maybe you are sitting in a coffee shop when a woman starts to giggle with uncontrollable laughter. In any of these scenarios, watch, observe, and learn. Capitalize on the experience of any situation of heightened interest.

Variable:

Take out a history book or a book that is full of pictures and look for pictures that stand out. Perhaps there is a photo in which everyone is running away from a fire. Make a mental note of everything you see and the way people are reacting in the specific situation. You also can take the original activity and observe people doing mundane tasks such as putting sugar in their coffee, tying their shoelaces, or taking money out of their pocket. Notice the differences in the ways people behave when performing these mundane and monotonous tasks.

Discussion:

What surprised you about the reactions you saw?

How did you decide when something was of profound interest?

What did you learn about human nature from this activity?

Do you think people act differently in heightened situations? Explore and justify your answer.

Purpose:

To observe how people react in heightened situations

In this exercise you get to see how people react in some sort of heightened event. You will most likely see some sort of unpredictable behavior. Perhaps you will see something that you never thought would happen in a situation such as this. Let's say that you are a very safe driver — you always look in your mirror and check your blind spot. Your friends have commented in the past on how safe and secure they feel when you drive. Today is a different story; you are extremely late for work, and you have a very important presentation to give. Now, you get in your car and drive off at breakneck speed hardly looking in your mirror, and at one point you almost run a red light. You see that when we are in extreme situations, our behavior can totally change. This is a huge note for your characters in plays or movies. If you have defined your character as cool, calm, and laid back, it does not mean this is the case in every situation. You need to evaluate your choices and decide: is this how my character would really react or respond? In Shakespeare's *Macbeth,* the aforementioned character says, "Present fears are less than horrible imaginings; my thought, whose murder yet is but fantastical, shakes so my single state of man that function is smother'd in surmise, and nothing is but what is not."[3] At the start of the play Macbeth is a hero, and by the end of it he is a cold-blooded murderer. If you create a one-dimensional character, you have most likely created someone who does not exist in the real world.

To build a tool box and wealth of resources

As you get used to making this observational tool a part of your everyday life, you will find that your understanding of human nature will grow stronger. You will have more resources from which to pull and use as building blocks for scenes or projects. Let's say you are playing a character who is getting fired from her job. You remember a situation from a couple of years ago when you witnessed a young lady having a shouting match with her boss. It is not the exact same situation, but perhaps there is something there that you can use, something you remember that will help you further your own scene. Five seconds ago I watched a man coming into the coffee shop looking for his wallet and then start to grin when he could not find it. He has just dashed back to his car. Why would he grin when he could not find his wallet? It is these interesting quirks in human nature that are the gems that flavor your acting.

[3]William Shakespeare and Roma Gill, ed., *Macbeth* (London: Oxford University Press, 1977), 9.

17. Spy Games

This is a fascinating exercise that I have utilized with a number of actors. Rent a movie related to espionage or the spy industry. Find a documentary that interviews former spies and those who are or have been involved in this secretive industry. You will probably find that most of these documentaries are based on what happened ten, twenty, or thirty years ago. Watch the documentary and read the body language of those being interviewed. Work out the subtext of their message. For instance, let's say a former spy is asked, "Did you photograph the files?" and the agent replies, "I was not even in the country at the time." Try to decide whether they are telling the truth. What brought you to that conclusion? Perhaps you see a nervous twitch, a glance to the ceiling, or a scratching of the head. One of the most fascinating parts of this activity is that almost all of the people you watch will be expert liars. They will know more about the ability to conceal the truth than most. There will be some who have the ability to beat a polygraph test. They will know more about body language and how to manipulate it than most actors will ever know. Therefore, relish the opportunity to learn from these great masters of the mind and body and learn as much from them as you can. Make notes on your observations and share them with friends or other actors and see if they come to the same conclusions.

Variables:

Do this same activity by watching interviews with politicians. Read their body language, the subtext of what they are saying, and draw some conclusions on their believability.

Discussion:

What was the most profound discovery you made when watching this documentary?

How would you differentiate the artful ability to lie with the actor's ability to recreate truth?

What are the lessons to be learned from observing body language?

How did the phrase, "truth is stranger than fiction" apply when you watched the documentary?

Purpose:

To utilize all resources around you for your acting

One aspect I have always found intriguing about this activity is that actors will often say that they were amazed at the acting ability of those they saw on the documentary. This may sound strange, but when you think about it, it's really quite logical. When an actor plays a role, he does so with various intentions such as bringing truth to the character, paying the bills, and being adored by his audience and fans. I would love it if actors' work was purely based on the love for acting, but this is neither practical nor realistic. When a spy or secret agent plays a role, he does so with a different level of purpose and intent. In some situations, if he fails to portray his character correctly, he may lose his life or face a lengthy prison sentence. The stakes are therefore very high, bringing new meaning to the phrase, "playing the role of your life." These pseudo-actors, therefore, become very committed to each role they play. I am not suggesting that all actors should go out and become spies, but I am suggesting that you do your research and homework for each role you play. Even if money and fame are powerful motivators for you, your desire to get the truth across through your character and his actions are, at the very least, equally as important. The ability to create truth is a powerful gift that needs to be developed and nurtured over time.

To understand human nature

In this exercise you are asked to study and delve into the psyche of some of the cleverest minds out there. Why these people do what they do could be linked to a number of passionate motivators such as power, money, excitement, and love for their country. As you start to discover more about what makes them tick, you learn more about their nature. As an actor, it is not only important for you to know what people do, but also why they do what they do. The motivation behind the act is usually far more interesting than the act itself.

Understanding human nature relates to what is considered acceptable behavior at a precise moment in history. While discussing England's Elizabethan period, Harrop and Epstein explain that, "Criminals were not only hanged in public but also cut into quarters."[4] To begin to understand human nature is an amazing feat in itself. This is going to put you in an excellent position to begin delving into your characters and seeing them as multidimensional.

---

[4]John Harrop and Sabin R. Epstein, *Acting with Style* (New York: Prentice Hall, 1990), 40.

18. Broken Heart

This is an activity you are going to love to hate. You can only do this exercise when you have a broken heart. The next time you're in a relationship that — for whatever reason — comes to an end, observe your own behavior. You may find that you have lost your appetite or that the food you eat has no taste. You might discover that you can't concentrate on anything and that you're walking around in a daze. One minute you think you are fine and the next minute you burst into tears. Sporadic and impulsive crying is not easy to create, yet you will probably find it a breeze at the time of this exercise. I'm not asking you to think about this situation in the future so you can cry; rather, observe the organic way in which your tears literally seem to come out of nowhere — or do they? You have to be your own judge here. Do you find that suddenly your life feels hollow and empty? Do all the important things in your world suddenly seem meaningless and insignificant? Has your behavior become unpredictable and sporadic? Regardless of what feelings you experience, the important thing is to take note of what is happening to you. Notice that I asked you to work this activity when your heart is broken and not simply when you are breaking up with someone. I know this is a challenging activity, but no one said you were working in an easy profession.

Variables:

Do this same exercise the first moment you realize you are in love.

Discussion:

How difficult has it been to work this activity while you are actually going through this pain?

Are there observations that you made in the moment that would not be possible to make at any other time?

Explore the possibility that extreme situations can totally change human behavior?

Why is love so complex?

Purpose:

To understand how extreme circumstances affect human behavior

The reason that I am asking you to do this exercise with a broken heart is because this is an extreme situation. At a time such as this it can be hard to think straight even if it's only for a short period of time. In this type of situation you may find that you are acting totally contradictory to your normal behavior. Perhaps you are a clean freak, and this week your apartment is an absolute mess. Maybe you love to exercise, and this week you haven't been able to work out. In other words, your actions and behaviors have changed because of the given circumstances. Why do people act the way they do? Any human character you are playing is a complex human being. You may only have one line, but the character has a lifetime.

Being in the moment

Acting is about being in the moment. In this exercise you are certainly in the moment in a very raw sense. You are not reviewing a broken heart at a later date; rather, you are in the very thick of the experience. You are going through these devastating feelings, and nothing is more real than that. In your acting there is time for reviewing and time for being. I will let you figure out what is relevant and when. In this exercise you are experiencing what it is to have loved and lost. As Leo Buscaglia observes, "A loving person recognizes needs. He needs people who care, someone who cares at least about him, who truly sees and hears him."[5]

19. Lights, Camera, Action!

For this exercise you need a home video camera. If you do not have one, borrow one from a friend. Prepare a monolog or scene that you like or have performed in the past. Set up your video camera to film yourself performing the scene or monolog. Once you have set your camera, take your time to get into position. Even though the camera is running, don't start your piece until you are ready. If you are doing a scene that calls for more than one person, simply say your lines and imagine the other person's responses. If you choose this approach, you should know the other character's lines, as well. Once you have recorded your piece, watch and critique it. Decide what worked and what didn't. It won't help you grow to simply say, "I Sucked!" Rather, you might say, "My lines sounded somewhat robotic because I was trying to remember them," "I didn't seem to know what to do with my hands," "I did a good job of telling the story," and/or "I understood the subtext of the scene."

[5]Leo Buscaglia, *Love* (New York: Ballantine Books, 1982), 43.

Remember, a critique not only focuses on areas that need work but also on what worked well. Come up with as many areas to critique as you can and then rehearse your scene, working on the areas you critiqued, off-camera before filming it a second time. Then watch and critique your second take.

Variables:

Work with specific camera framing such as head and shoulders only or full body within a small, contained area. Or simply record your voice and listen to yourself. You will most likely find that you sound quite different from your own perception of yourself.

Discussion:

Did you give yourself enough time to complete this exercise?
Would it work just as well if you broke it up over a couple of days?
What are the challenges with directing your own scene?
Is there any value in reviewing your own on-camera work?

Purpose:

To see and review your own work

Some actors never want to watch their own work, and others watch all of their work. This is entirely up to you; however, it is interesting to note that if we were living in the nineteenth century, you would not have had this option available. Seeing yourself on camera might open up a whole new can of worms for you, but if it allows you to grow, then it is of value. It can also be quite powerful to critique your own work instead of always relying on the opinions of others.

To work with the medium of television and film

You might say that you only want to work on the stage because this is where the true art of acting lies. The challenge is that if you want to make a living as an actor, you are most likely going to work in the television and film industry at some stage in your career. This isn't true for everybody, but in monetary terms it may be a reality you have to face. It is also worth noting that if you want to reach a wider audience, you are going to have to work in television or film. The Greeks could reach audiences of many thousands in their theatrical performances. Today we are able to reach audiences of many millions, if not billions. This is a powerful medium that actors cannot ignore.

Chapter 4
Balance and Neutrality

20. Silence Is Golden

Take six hours and be totally silent — no singing, no laughing, no chatting on the phone. For six hours, live in an inner world of silence. You are more than welcome to go out and about in your life, but do not talk to anyone. Do not mouth words or start writing notes on pieces of paper. Be an observer of life and stay with your inner thoughts. You may choose to do this exercise entirely at home without coming into contact with anyone. You have probably completed this exercise a number of times in your life without even considering it, but now that you are aware of your assignment it will feel very different from past experiences. Feel free to write, listen to music, read books, or whatever you would like to do. At the six-hour mark, strike up a conversation with someone and notice how your world has readjusted. This exercise should last no less than six hours, but it may go on for as long as you like.

Variables:

Be silent for six hours, only this time go to a place where there is absolutely no sound but the sound of nature. For the next six hours not only will you be silent, but so will the world around you.

Discussion:

You have heard the expression, "Silence is golden." Is there any truth to this?

What was the most amazing discovery you made through this exercise?

How does silence play a role in the life of an actor?

In what way were your senses heightened through this activity?

Purpose:

To appreciate the internal and external worlds of the actor

In this exercise you can take out all of the clutter in your life. There is no one to talk to, so you get to live your life a little bit differently. You will probably find that you become more aware of your inner thoughts, and you can monitor these. It may give you a newfound respect for the way the inner chatter of your mind continues on a regular basis. You might find that you start to work on or explore activities that you wouldn't normally do. Perhaps you're not a reader, but today you spend an hour reading a book. As an actor, it is important to stretch your boundaries on a continual basis.

This activity also has external value. If you choose to go outside and mingle, you are going to find that your powers of observation have increased. You'll find that your listening skills have become more heightened. I will let you decide what value this has to you as an actor. I hope that once you have completed this activity, you find the desire to put aside time for silence on a regular basis. Once you have completed this exercise, for practical reasons you might find that one hour is easier to work with in the future.

To develop your level of discipline

Completing this exercise in its entirety will require discipline. If you say one word after three hours and stay silent for the rest of the time, then you have done well; however, you will not have completed the exercise. This activity is an excellent metaphor for actors because it highlights the absolute need for discipline in your profession. Let's say you're asked to arrive on set with your lines learned for a scene you were given the night before. This is no easy task. As you arrive on set, you have only memorized half of your lines, but you figure it will be okay. It is not okay, and you make error after error. Because of you it takes an extra eight takes to shoot the scene. Because of your lack of discipline you may find your acting career cut drastically short. Please remember that all of the people you come into contact with are only human, and they will respond in the way that humans do. Discipline is such an important part of your chosen profession that if you don't have any, you need to get some, and fast. The concept behind this book is not only to enhance your acting abilities, but also to see you become a working actor.

21. Jugolog

This activity works in two parts. For the first part you'll need a monolog that you have already learned and used for audition/agent purposes. For the second part, acquire some juggling balls, apples, oranges, tennis balls, or whatever takes your fancy.

Work on your monolog for ten or fifteen minutes. Go through it, perform it, and if you feel the desire to make any adjustments go ahead and do so. When your monolog is prepared, put it aside and start to focus on the juggling. You can choose how many balls to work with, but make sure you challenge yourself. If four balls are very easy for you, then you should juggle five or more. Spend ten or fifteen minutes working with the balls and getting comfortable.

Now, integrate the two pieces together. Work your monolog and juggle simultaneously. Make sure you are committing seriously to both tasks. I have seen a number of actors juggle balls and recite their lines verbatim, but this is not the aim of the exercise. Perform your monolog with all the intensity, passion, and feelings you can muster while at the same time focusing your energy on juggling the balls to the best of your ability. Don't juggle the balls and continue to drop them as if it is no big deal; you must do your very best not to drop a single ball. If you drop the balls, pick them up and keep going. Do not stop your monolog, but continue in an organic fashion. Do this exercise at least three times so that you fully experience it. Once you have finished, perform your monolog one more time without juggling and see if it has changed in any way.

Variables:

Give yourself a different task to complete — a task that takes a great deal of focus and concentration — while you work your monolog.

Discussion:

What was the most noticeable difference between performing the monolog on its own and performing it while juggling?

What was the most frustrating part of this exercise?

How did this activity connect the physical and mental processes for you?

At any point did you feel like giving up on this activity? What kept you going?

Purpose:

To free yourself within the work

At first glance this exercise may feel quite restricting. You are unable to focus on one task or the other, but must be engaged in both. This in itself is quite freeing because at some point you will have to momentarily put trust in yourself to allow the monolog to flow. You will also have to be free enough to allow yourself to continue to juggle while your focus is on the monolog. This is freeing because you cannot continuously focus on only one of the tasks if you are to succeed in the other. The freer you are in the work as an actor, the more room you will have to make discoveries. If you are open to new possibilities, then your acting has great potential for growth. Oftentimes, an actor must put on the same performance each and every night. This is difficult because you are a different person today than the one who performed yesterday. You have had new experiences today that have subtly changed you. Your performance will always be slightly different each night, even if in a very minute way.

To develop multitasking abilities

In this exercise you have to perform two tasks simultaneously. As an actor, you are going to have to multitask on a continual basis. You have to know your lines, know your blocking, know your objectives and motivations, remember your props, hit your marks, be listening to the other actors, and so on. You also have to juggle the business aspects of your career. You have to focus on sending out headshots and resumés, connecting with your agent/manager, taking acting classes, working your other job, exploring networking opportunities, building your own website, being proactive on auditions, etc. The actor's life is one of constant multitasking, and the more you get used to this concept, the smoother the journey will be.

22. Work In/Work Out

This exercise is simple yet fundamental. Work out every week. Your workout doesn't have to be going to the gym or running around the park; it can be anything that takes your fancy. Perhaps you could go walking in your neighborhood. You might be a person who enjoys riding your bicycle, going hiking, or rock climbing. You can really use your imagination here. Let's say you enjoy shopping. You may go and walk around the mall for two hours. This will be great exercise, just remember to leave your credit card at home. It is key that you find something you enjoy doing. Whatever you choose, introduce exercise into your life from this moment on. For those who do not exercise regularly, this will be quite a challenge.

I call this "Work In/Work Out" because working out should be part of an actor's work. Allow exercise to become part of your lifestyle. You may say that you cannot afford the time to do this; I say you cannot afford not to. Start to observe how exercise starts to make your body feel different and how you feel different about yourself.

Variables:
Change up your exercise routine to suit your desires and needs.

Discussion:
Do you find that exercise helps enhance your mood?

What technique are you using to guide yourself in making exercise part of your lifestyle?

Why may exercise be more important for actors than it is for most professions?

How does exercise encourage you to review your time management?

Purpose:
To appreciate your body as your instrument
You have heard people say that their body is their temple; for the actor, your body is your instrument. You need to understand how to play it and make it work in a multitude of different directions. If your body is totally out of shape, you are harming and abusing the only selling point you have as an actor — yourself. I am not necessarily talking about size; a person can be slim and still have high blood pressure. I am also not suggesting that all actors should look like clones, rather that you should respect your most valuable possession. The work of an actor can be incredibly grueling, so being in shape is going to give you the extra edge you need. It is always sad to read of an actor (or anyone) whose life ended prematurely as a result of an unhealthy lifestyle. Get yourself moving in the right direction so that you can have a career that is not only successful but also long and enduring.

To put your body in a state of balance
Homeostasis means putting the body back into balance, which is precisely where we want our minds and bodies to be. As you complete this exercise, you will feel more grounded, more centered, and generally more relaxed. This may not always be the case if, for instance, you are lifting heavy weights. But if you follow your weight-lifting with the sauna steam room, you will still achieve a state of balance. The closer you can come to living in a state of balance, the better. When you are balanced, ideas will come to you and your creative juices will flow more easily. Exercise is one more step on the way to making this possible.

23. On Your Marks, Get Set, Go!

Run the hundred-yard dash. If you don't have the opportunity to go to an athletic track, find a stretch of grass that is about one hundred yards.

Before you actually run, be sure to warm up so you don't pull a muscle. Think about and visualize the race ahead in its different stages. Close your eyes and imagine yourself moving around, loosening up, getting in the start position, running the race at an incredible speed, and finishing feeling alive and fresh and invigorated.

Now follow through with these actions. Walk around and loosen up your body until you feel comfortable and ready. Get into a starting position. This is a race against yourself. Run the fastest possible hundred yards you can; you only have one attempt to do so. On your marks: put all of your concentration and focus into what you are about to do. Get set: you should now be alert and ready with all of your energy about to propel you forward. Go: unleash yourself into your hundred-yard dash as if nothing can hold you back. Run as fast as you possibly can. When you have finished, take a few minutes to recover. Walk around and notice the difference in how you are feeling now as opposed to how you felt just before the race began.

Variables:

Do this same exercise with a hundred-yard swim.

Discussion:

Did you feel like adrenaline was pumping through your body before the race?

What was going on the moment just before you unleashed yourself out of the blocks?

When you were running, was there any point at which you felt like you could not stop?

What does running a race have to do with acting?

Purpose:

To give a metaphor for preparation in acting

In this exercise you had to prepare before running the race. With stretching, mobility exercises, visualizations, and generally psyching yourself up, you may end up running a better race. Likewise, an actor needs to prepare for each and every performance. I don't want to tell you exactly how you should prepare because it's not an exact science, but you should prepare, nonetheless. It is true that some actors will literally be joking around one minute and then be filming a very dramatic and moving scene the next. It is also true that movies that have been purely improvised have won Oscars, so there may not have been a great deal of importance on preparation. What I would question here is with what consistency these types of performances can be mustered up. Acting is an art form that requires preparation if it is to reach its true potential.

To experience the unknown

When you are running the race at your top speed, there is a potential moment in which you could not pull back or stop even if you wanted to. It is as if you are falling off a cliff with no reins to pull you back. In that moment, you are experiencing the unknown, even if only for a split second. For an actor, to step into the unknown during a performance can create an inspirational moment, compelling in nature. While these moments can be fleeting, this shouldn't stop the actor from striving for them. Likewise, actors shouldn't try to live completely in the unknown. If you were stepping into the unknown every moment of your performance, you might fall off the stage or bash your head into the camera.

24. Pranayama

Pranayama is the generic name for breath work. In this exercise we are going to explore some of the ideas behind the breath. I am not going to teach you breath work in specific detail — for that you should take classes, read specific books, or watch a video.

For this exercise, take in some very short, sharp, and rapid breaths through your mouth. Do this for about fifteen seconds. Notice the physical and mental affect it has on your body. Do you feel stressed? Are you dizzy? Has your level of anxiety risen? Do you feel more energized? Do you feel more calm and relaxed? Do you feel more focused? Did you have an emotional release such as bursting out in tears? Now do the same breathing pattern, except this time breathe through your nose. Again, observe how this affects you mentally and physically. Now take long deep breaths through your mouth for about thirty seconds. Then do the same thing through your nose. Observe the effects of both.

The purpose of this exercise is to become aware of your breath and the effect it has on the way you think and feel. I want to remind you that we have not hit the technical aspects of breath work in this exercise — for that you are going to want to further your training.

Variables:

See Exercise 37: Vibrations (page 77).

Discussion:

Do you think people can develop holding patterns in their breathing?

Can your breathing cause muscular tensions in your body?

Can your breathing encourage the release of chemicals such as adrenaline, endorphins, cortical, and lactic acid?

How important is it to understand breath in the actor's work?

Purpose:

To understand how breath can influence your physical and mental state

In this exercise you are given very simple examples of how breath can influence your state. Therefore, controlling your breathing is of value to you as an actor. What if you are playing the role of a king who is supposed to display a great deal of power and control? If, because you are feeling stressed and nervous, you are breathing shallowly, you will be contradicting your character's persona. As Gay Hendricks puts it, "The process of breathing, if fully understood and experienced in its profound significance, could teach us more than all the philosophies in the world."[1] If you aren't aware of the capability of breath, it can work against you on a regular basis. By understanding breath, you can train it to work in your favor and manipulate it to your advantage.

To explore the specifics of acting

In this exercise we are looking at the breath, which some actors will tell you has nothing whatsoever to do with acting. I would agree that, for poor and mediocre acting, these people may well be right. What we are talking about here, though, is acting that matters and has some value. This acting takes a great deal of work on your behalf and will

---

[1]Gay Hendricks, *The Art of Breathing and Centering* (Los Angeles, CA: St. Martin's Press, 1989), 3.

develop and grow over time. This type of acting demands that the actor continue to make new discoveries and ask questions. The bottom line is that acting of value requires work and attention to detail. It is also worth noting that while acting takes a great deal of work, it should appear effortless to the audience.

Chapter 5
Concentration and Focus

25. Lace Up

For this exercise you need to wear a pair of lace up shoes. Untie the laces on both shoes. I know it sounds strange, but stick with me here. Now tie your shoelaces in the most perfect fashion possible. Imagine you are being watched by a casting director and this is an audition for a big commercial that could make you an obscene amount of money. When you tie your shoes, remember that you are not allowed to make one mistake or fumble; the tying of the laces has to be perfect. Once you have completed your task, take a moment to admire your work, then untie your shoelaces again.

This time, while you tie your shoes, make a mental note of all the things you have to accomplish this week. Think about those things with absolute precision. What is the first thing you are going to get done today, what is the next thing you have to do, at what time and where? The most important part of this activity is to recall in detail the tasks you need to complete. For example, "I have to take my car into Ted's Mechanics at three this afternoon to get the oil changed." Don't pay any special attention to your shoelaces; just get them tied at the same time as you are completing your list of tasks.

Once you are finished, let everything you have just done sink in. Think about how you acted in the first half of this activity when tying your laces was of paramount importance. Compare this to how much attention you paid to tying your shoelaces in the second half of the activity when they were of secondary importance.

Variables:

Work this exercise by getting yourself dressed from top to bottom, using the same premise as before. Complete the task of getting dressed as though it were of utter importance, and then add the to-do list the second time.

Discussion:

Why do you need to be aware of economy of effort as an actor?

Is it possible to focus your attention on more than one task at the same time?

Did you sense any changes when your primary focus became the "to do" list?

What are the benefits of working with this exercise on a consistent basis?

Purpose:

To understand direction of focus

In the first part of this activity you were asked to focus solely on the task of tying your shoelaces. In fact, this activity was made to be of paramount importance as if nothing else mattered. The challenge is that in the vast majority of situations the task of tying your shoelaces is an automatic process in which very little focus or concentration is needed. A number of actors will put a great deal of attention and focus into a simple task on-stage because they want to "get it right." As a result, the task will often appear forced or unrealistic. A simple task rarely demands our attention unless there are external circumstances (such as a job interview or going on a date) that dictate otherwise. In the second part of this activity, your attention is divided by adding a to-do list, which takes your mind off your shoelaces. It forces you to make the tying of the shoelaces less of a priority, allowing a simple task made difficult to become a less important task once again. This activity will help you have a clearer understanding of focus of attention.

To understand economy of effort

I am going to go out on a limb now and say that many human beings are somewhat lazy. By that I mean that if there is a shorter or quicker way of doing something, we generally will choose it. An actor who attaches too much importance to a simple task (without justification) will also most likely exert too much energy. In the second part of this activity you have too much to do to exert all the energy into the tying of the shoelaces, and therefore you have to utilize the principle of economy of effort. This also will help you relate to situations in everyday life when most of us are constantly looking for ways to save time and work more efficiently. Anyone who knows how to do something well will exert an economy of effort. If you look at the street sweepers, you will see that they have learned how to do their job most efficiently so they can exert less energy. Look at the bank teller counting money and watch the efficient way he is able to do this. The more repetitious a task in our day-to-day lives, the more economy of effort we learn to exert.

26. Hold 'Em

This is a very simple exercise that can have very interesting results. Try this exercise when you are out and about visiting friends. Let's say your friend is sitting at the other end of the room. Call her name; when she looks at you, see how long you can hold her attention without saying another word. How long are you able to maintain eye contact? Your aim is to hold eye contact for five to eight seconds. This is easier said than done. Once eye contact is broken, start a conversation so that your friend does not think you've totally lost it.

Try this exercise in different environments such as a house, coffee shop, and nightclub. See if you can hold someone's attention just as well in a noisy environment as in a quiet setting. Once you lose eye contact, the activity is over.

You can also use this activity with people you do not know by saying something like, "Excuse me," and continuing the activity as before. Please use common sense when using activities such as this with people you do not know. Be respectful and always have an out. For example, you may say, "Excuse me" to someone in a grocery store. Once the eye contact ends, ask, "Can you tell me where I can find the tomatoes?" You don't want to turn around and tell a perfect stranger, "Ha, ha, I got you!" Using common sense is an important part of being an actor, so get used to it.

Variables:

There are a couple of ways to vary this exercise. After you call out a friend's name, get his attention and lose it, wait two or three minutes and do it again. In the space of the next fifteen minutes see if you can maintain eye contact three or four times. Be careful; by the end of this activity he may not want to be your friend anymore.

To try this exercise with an extra twist, when you call someone's name out, mispronounce it so that Sarah becomes Farah or Lara. See if you are still able to hold her attention in the same manner. You'll be surprised at how many people don't pick up on your mispronunciation of their names.

Discussion:

How challenging is it to hold someone's attention for five to eight seconds?

Why is it important to work off the other actors in any scene you are in?

What does it mean to act and react?

Why is it important for an actor to have confidence and courage?

Purpose:

To infect your partner

In this exercise you are attempting to hold another individual's eye contact. This takes a tremendous amount of energy on your part to ignite enough interest in them to hold your gaze. As an actor, you are constantly in a position of having to give your fellow actors enough to be able to bounce off you. Let's say you're playing a teenager in high school who hates school and tells her teacher she is dropping out because, "School sucks!" If there's not enough intensity coming from you, there will be no tension in this scene, and the teacher will be responding from a weaker position. When you start this exercise, you have to give everything you can in order to hold a gaze, and so it should be in each and every scene. Develop this tool, as it allows your intensity and energy to infuse the other actors engaged with you.

To build courage and confidence

One of the biggest challenges I find with actors is that they lack confidence and courage. Instead of believing in themselves, too many actors feel insecure and need the constant approval of others. This is dangerous because people's opinions can be fleeting and subjective. It takes guts to turn to someone, hold his gaze continually, and say nothing. As you build your confidence in activities such as these, you also give yourself a new set of references for what you are capable of doing. In my book, *112 Acting Games*, I say, "If you foster your students' belief in their own potential then anything is possible."[1] It is so important that actors be confident and believe in themselves because there are going to be many people along the road who will not believe.

27. Concentration Zone

Gather up some of your acting work. Perhaps you have lines that you are learning for a play, movie, or scene study class. Maybe you need to do a lot of research on a character's background. Perhaps you are researching agents to send your resumé to, or perhaps you are doing

[1]Gavin Levy, *112 Acting Games* (Colorado Springs, CO: Meriwether Publishing, 2005), 146.

mail outs for auditions. Choose one or all of the above, or something completely different — the main stipulation is that it be something related to acting that requires your focus and concentration.

Take yourself to a very busy and loud environment, such as a coffee shop. Go somewhere that is going to make it very difficult for you to concentrate. This is a very important part of the exercise, so if the place you go to is not as noisy as you thought, go somewhere else. Next, begin your work. If you choose to learn your lines, sit there and, even if you find it impossible to concentrate, continue with the task of learning your lines. (Normally I would never suggest that you sit down while learning your lines, but for the sake of this activity, it is okay.)

Working on your task is only half of your assignment. The other half is that you work on your project clearly, calmly, and proficiently. This is going to be easier said than done; you're going to have to develop some very clear methods of concentration and focus to see you through. Let's say you complete your task but are stressed because of all the noise and racket going on around you. If this is the case, you have only completed half of the exercise. By the time you finish, you should be calm, relaxed, and focused, regardless of all the noise around you. When you are finished, review what just happened and be honest with yourself on how well you did.

Variables:

Take the same task and work in a place of absolute silence such as a museum or a library, and see how the results differ this time.

Discussion:

What is the relevance of this activity for the actor?

Did you find a place that was kind of noisy or extremely noisy?

What was the biggest obstacle you found in getting your task done? What methods did you use to overcome this dilemma?

Purpose:

To enhance your levels of concentration and focus

This exercise immediately brings your attention to the fact that as actors we need to have excellent levels of focus and concentration. I wanted you to go out into the real world so that you could get a real-world experience. Let's say you are on the set of a movie. As they are about to shoot the scene, you may here the director say, "Quiet on set!" This is the very moment before filming, but what about all the moments before that? In between takes you will have light crews, makeup artists, wardrobe crews, stunt doubles, producers, gaffers, sound technicians, and other actors running all around. Through all of this you need to stay calm and focused on your scene and your character-driven motivations. Even if someone is dabbing makeup on your face or taking in the seam on your dress, you need to stay absolutely focused. If you are in a play, you may feel that this does not apply because the audience is normally respectful and quiet. However, it is amazing how many actors like to have a good old chinwag backstage. You have to find a way to separate yourself from these situations or politely diffuse any potential conversations, lest they take away from your acting preparation. There are many people involved in a project that have jobs to do; they need to get tasks done in their own manner. As an actor, your work requires different levels of discipline and focus, and you need to be aware of these principles and adhere to them.

To encourage you to practice your skills

In this exercise you are put in a position where you have to develop your concentration and focus skills or else getting your task done will be virtually impossible or incredibly time consuming. You are purposely propelled into this situation in order to develop these skills. An actor will sometimes say, "I wish I could concentrate more," "I wish I was a better actor," or "I wish I could do accents." In all these cases I would say, yes, yes, and yes. If you are willing to practice and do the work, there is no reason why you can't enhance all areas of your acting. Sometimes it's as if we want things to happen by magic — we want the goods, but we don't want to do the work to get there. It's also the case that some actors will look at another person and say, "They just have it, and so do I." This is a limiting belief and quite often not the case. When my mum was in college, she had a friend who would party every night — he was a real social animal. He was also a top student. My mother, on the other hand, would study very hard, party only on a limited basis, and struggle to get good grades. I remember her telling me that people were amazed at how naturally intelligent her friend was. Years later, she learned that this young man had gone home each night after partying and studied for hours (apparently he didn't sleep much). The next time you meet a "natural talent," don't be so sure; there is a tremendous amount of practice and dedication that goes into becoming a "natural talent."

28. Perfect

For this exercise you need a pencil and a piece of poster paper that is three feet long. You also need either a ruler, a measuring tape, or possibly a piece of string. This exercise is both very simple and very complex all at the same time.

Draw a line that is one yard in length. Your line should be exactly one yard and absolutely straight for the entire length. If it is slightly slanted at one point, then it is not a perfect line. If there is a slight break in the middle where you moved the ruler, it is not a perfect line. If it is one millimeter off, it is not a perfect line. You job is to make a perfectly straight, one-yard line.

If you use a pencil you can start again as many times as you need to. Have patience for this activity, and do not give up. This exercise is based on a picture on display at a famous gallery in London. It is of a perfect line, and is worth thousands upon thousands of dollars.

Variables:

Come up with your own.

Discussion:

Why is this activity so much harder that it initially appears?

How do you define a perfect line?

Does perfection have a place in acting? How would you define perfection in acting?

Purpose:

To explore the concept of perfection

In this exercise you are asked to draw a perfect line. While it is very simple to draw a line, it is quite another matter to draw a perfect line. This is an excellent metaphor when talking about acting. It is fairly easy to learn your lines and sound like you know what you are doing. You could create a mediocre performance and still be somewhat entertaining. But to truly move your audience, to be an actor that can transcend a deeper message and have a true understanding of the craft of acting, is a quite complex task. Such an actor will spend many years learning, growing, making mistakes, and learning and growing some more. The actor should never stop learning. To say there is perfection in acting is too subjective, and yet there are performances that we will never forget. There are performances that stop us in our tracks and leave us speechless. Drawing a perfect line could take years; becoming an actor of substance could likewise take many years of dedication and hard work.

To develop patience

When you start this exercise you may find that you very quickly become discouraged. This, in turn, can try your patience and make you want to give up. When you are rehearsing a role, you may find there are times when nothing is going right. You don't understand the character, you cannot find your motivation for the scene, and your fellow actor never wants to rehearse. Perhaps you don't understand your character yet, but as you work through the role you will find that you develop ideas to enhance your understanding. By being patient you allow your mind to remain in a creative state. If you are getting mad and frustrated, you will find that your mind becomes saturated in these negative thoughts. If you have an acting partner who does not want to rehearse the scenes with you and you lose your temper, he will want to work with you even less. Even though he is the one being unprofessional, you must stay professional at all times. Ask him politely when would be a good time to get together. This does not guarantee success, but it gives you a better chance of achieving your goal. As an actor, it serves to be a pragmatist because situations will constantly come up that demand a creative approach.

29. Book Bytes

Pick up some sort of fiction book that has fairly small print. This should be a book that you have not read before. Flip to a random page in the book and read that page silently to yourself. At the same time, think about something completely different. You could think about a vacation you had last year, what you are going to do over the weekend, or a movie you saw recently. Whatever you choose, put a great deal of your focus and attention on it while reading the book.

Now read the page again, and this time put your full attention on the book. When you have finished the page, reflect on what you remember about the story you have just read — not necessarily facts, just the general story. Compare this to what you remember from the first reading. I did not ask you to do this the first time because now that I have mentioned it, you know exactly what you can remember from that occasion.

Variables:

Watch a scene in a movie twice. Think of something else the first time and then focus on the scene in the movie the second time.

Discussion:

Were you surprised at how little/much you remembered on the first occasion?

On which occasion did you enjoy reading the book more?

How do listening skills relate to this exercise?

Did the time of day you worked this exercise have any effects on your findings?

Purpose:

To highlight the importance of focus and concentration

It is quite possible that on the first occasion you read the page you remembered virtually nothing. While this may seem unimportant, compare it to your acting. Imagine you are in a scene where you are unfocused because you are trying to remember your next line or plan what you are going to have for dinner tonight. Your acting will seem disconnected because, simply put, it is disconnected — you have no idea what is going on in the scene. You might argue that you know exactly what is going on because you have played the scene many times before, but I am going to argue that in that precise moment you are disconnected from the scene. This is not the same as appearing somewhat unfocused because of specific choices made by the character. Concentration and focus are an important part of the actor's work in many facets.

To understand the bigger picture

In this exercise I did not ask you to see how many facts you could remember, rather I wanted you to think of the overall story that you had just read. Get used to the idea that whether you are in a play, a movie, or even a commercial, there is always some form of story being told. Some of the actors I work with will receive small roles or non-speaking roles, and at times they choose not to do anything more than look at their specific scene. They argue that their character would not know anything more than this, so why should they? There is truth to this sometimes. There are times when it may be to your advantage to not know what follows. However, there are also times when this is sheer laziness. Apply this exercise to your work as you see fit. Decide on the merits of understanding the overarching story of whatever project you are involved in.

Chapter 6
Nonverbal Communication

30. Poet and You Know It

This exercise is a favorite with actors, and yet it is also challenging. Choose a poem or a song you know. Next, think of an emotional event in your life, perhaps breaking up with a boyfriend, failing an exam, losing a pet, or having an argument with your father. Don't choose a traumatic experience. (It is important to remember that while acting classes offer room for exploration and growth, they are not therapy classes, and your acting instructor is not your therapist.) Now tell the story of this emotional event, but with a twist. Tell the story using the words of the poem or song you chose. Pour your heart out using these words and these words alone. Be careful not to sing your song or fall into its rhythm. The idea is tell your story through these very specific words, not to sing it. While these are the only words you have, the words are not truly important; they are merely a vehicle for you to fully express your emotional event. This can be quite emotionally draining, so be sure to choose the right time to complete this exercise.

Variables:

Take a different emotional experience and express it through dance. Choose a specific type of dance, perhaps ballet, jazz, tap, or salsa. The experience needs to come through your dance; it is very important for you to get that message across.

Discussion:

What discoveries did you make during this exercise?

How different did it feel to tell your story using someone else's words?

How do you feel about using your own experiences in your acting? Is this a help or a hindrance?

What does the phrase, "we are the sum of all our experiences," mean to the actor?

Purpose:

Understanding how to convey the subtext

In this exercise you have an underlying message that you must get across with words that do not relate to the actual circumstances. The subtext of what we are saying can often fit into this category. A friend may ask you how your day is going, and you may say, "excellent," but the subtext may tell us that you are having a really bad day. Or perhaps a boyfriend tells his girlfriend, "I love you," but the subtext tells her he doesn't really mean this. People often say things they don't mean, and so will the characters you are playing. This is a great exercise to highlight this point to an extreme.

To work with body language and physicality

You don't have to make a conscious decision to explore your body language in this activity. If you are committed to the process, it will take on a life of its own. If you are exploring a past event where you lost a favorite dog, notice what happens to your body: do your shoulders sag, are you hunched over, is your voice shaky, are your feet turned in, are your arms crossed? After the exercise is complete, be specific in recalling what you have experienced physically. Body language is a huge part of what we do, and yet quite often actors will fail to explore or understand the power that body language has in communication. Julias Fast explains in his book, *Body Language*, "Body language and kinesics are based on the behavioral patterns of nonverbal communication."[1] If we realize that seventy percent of all our communication is conveyed through body language, we will begin to see the need to explore it more fully.

31. Conversation Starter

For this exercise, start a conversation with someone you don't know and see if you can read the subtext of what they are saying. For instance, you may choose to go to the grocery store and ask one of the staff if they can tell you where the peanut butter aisle is. He may reply, "It is in aisle three, on the left side, just above the strawberry jelly." Listen closely to the reply and try to garner what he is thinking. Perhaps he's thinking, "I have done this a million times before and it is really boring," or "Why can't this jerk go find out for himself instead of being so lazy?" He's not going to give you this information, so you have to read it from his response. Things to pay attention to are the tone of voice, the pitch of voice, eye contact, facial expression, body language, etc. Is he smiling? Is the smile real or forced? Are his arms folded or uncrossed?

[1]Julias Fast, *Body Language* (New York: Pocket Books, 1971), 1.

Is his breathing deep or shallow? Does he appear rushed, or does he have time to talk to you? These are just a few examples of clues to help you understand the subtext of what this person is really saying.

Remember, subtext is the hidden thoughts beneath the words we say. A boyfriend could tell his girlfriend, "I love you," and the subtext could be, "It's time for us to break up." When doing this exercise, make sure you're in a safe environment. Try this exercise with different people and make mental notes of the subtext of their words. You may never know if you are correct in your assessments; you are making a calculated guess. As you are talking, pay attention to your own subtext — what are you really saying?

Variables:

You can also utilize this exercise with friends. During a conversation, make mental notes of what you think they are really saying. At the end of the conversation explain to them what you were doing (choose a good friend), and see how much of what you came up with was correct.

Discussion:

What were your criteria for choosing the people to speak to?

How much did you learn about this person from paying attention to the subtext?

Why is subtext so important for the actor to utilize and understand?

Why do you think I had you go out in public for this activity?

Purpose:

To understand the real meaning of what is being said

This exercise asks you to discover what it is that people are really saying to you as opposed to the words that come out of their mouths. The more you practice this, the deeper an understanding you'll have of what people are really saying. If you are working on a film script, you'll find that you are often given very literal dialog. It is up to you as the actor to find the subtext and lift the words off the page. I cannot stress enough how important this is for the actor to comprehend. The subtext of a conversation is often far more interesting than the conversation itself. This activity will lead you to pay attention to your own subtext when you are having conversations with other people. One of my aims is to allow you to utilize your environment as a constant training ground for your acting.

To find curiosity in human nature

Another reason the subtext of a conversation is so important is that we are often saying things we don't really mean. When you go out in the morning you might bump into a neighbor who asks how you're doing. You say "Good, thanks," but what you are thinking is, "I've got to go to work, which really sucks because I can't stand my boss." You then proceed to ask your neighbor how she is doing. She says, "Just fine," but what she really wanted to say is, "I've got to find a way to pay all these bills, and could you please turn your music down lower at night?" It is often far easier to say something non-committal or give an automatic answer than to tell people how you really feel. It is also worth remembering that often people don't really have an interest in your answer; they are just making conversation. This is quite true in audition situations, as well; pay attention to the subtext behind what those auditioning you say.

32. Picture Perfect

Go get a number of different magazines. One might be a fashion magazine, another might be about housekeeping, and another may be about technology. Try to find magazines that contrast each other in some way. Make sure that each of these magazines has plenty of pictures of people, both in the articles and in the ads. Look at the different pictures of people and decide what it is they are really saying. For instance, you might find an advertisement with a man who is smiling and supposedly saying, "I am happy because I use such and such product." If you look closer, you might find that his smile does not turn up at the edges, his eyes look slightly glazed and dull, and his smile appears forced rather than soft and warm. Instead of being genuinely happy, this man is saying, "They have asked me to hold this pose forty times now, and I am really fed up with it." In other words, analyze the pictures for authenticity.

You can do this exercise with any pictures in the magazine that involve people — they do not have to be in an advertisement. In fact, it might be quite interesting to compare pictures in advertisements with regular pictures of people. Do you feel the regular people look more genuine? Perhaps they are nervous being in front of the camera and it shows. It is very important that you are specific in the way you define each picture. Saying, "I don't believe his expression," is not specific enough. Look at his eyes, his mouth, his arms, his shoulders, his feet, the tensions in his handshake, and make your observations. See if you can find three pictures that you believe to be totally genuine and three that seem totally fake and explain why. I have asked you to use contrasting magazines for balance and to take away any biases you might find in one magazine over another. You can show these pictures to other friends and see if they come to the same conclusions that you did.

Variables:

Look for pictures of animals and make similar observations. What is the cow really saying? You are not looking for a genuine cow or a fake cow, but try to read the cow's facial expressions and body language.

Discussion:

When you looked at a picture, did you stick with your first impression or find that the more specific you got the more your impressions were changed?

Did you find the pictures in one magazine to be more genuine than those in another? If so, what factors do you think play into this?

What were the major differences you found between the advertisement and the non-advertisement pictures?

Purpose:

To read body language

In this exercise you are paying particular attention to the nonverbal cues given by these pictures. In day-to-day life people are giving off nonverbal cues all the time. With any character you play you will want to access your nonverbal cues. This activity allows you to see the importance of body language as it applies to others. Get used to the idea of looking at other people and understanding what it is they are saying in contrast to what they think they are saying. As an actor, this is a very important distinction for you to make. You can be in a scene and be positive you are giving a certain performance when in fact the other actors and the audience are reading it completely differently. By understanding and interpreting the body language of others, you will be far more able to understand what your own body language is saying.

Acting lessons from life

The world is full of wonderful resources for you to take advantage of to enhance your understanding of human behavior. These magazines or newspapers were not necessarily produced for actors, and yet they give great examples of good and bad acting. They tell us so much about what the people in the photographs are thinking or not thinking. The best thing about the resources around you is that many are free or very cheap, and yet they offer invaluable lessons. To most people a magazine is just a magazine, but to an actor it is a valuable resource. Start looking around and discover what other valuable resources are out there.

33. Audience Reactions

For this exercise go to the theatre and watch a movie. When the movie is finished, stay in your seat and watch the audience leave. Pay attention to the atmosphere in the theatre at the end of the film. Get a sense of the impression that the movie made on the audience. Here are a few potential observations to get you started: are people talking as they leave? What are they saying? Are some people staying in their seats as the movie finishes and the credits come up? What is the general atmosphere in the theatre? Make sure that you are the very last person to leave the auditorium. As you enter the lobby you may hear more comments about the movie — see what you can pick up. Do this exercise on three occasions over an extended period of time. Perhaps you could see a comedy, a drama, and a romance movie. Go to the movies on different days and at different times so you can get a real cross-spectrum. I would prefer that for this exercise you work with large rather than small audiences so that you can get a grand sense of the audience reactions. Once you have finished, compare and review your findings. It will also be interesting if you compare your own reactions to the audience reactions.

Variables:

Do this same activity by going to see three plays.

Discussion:

Were you surprised by the audience reactions?

By staying until the very end, what was your most surprising discovery?

Were you able to predict the audience reactions?

In your opinion, can a comedy be just as profound as a drama?

Purpose:

To learn to appreciate your audience

A hundred years ago, this exercise might not have been as important. All actors performed in front of a live audience and got a sense of the way an audience felt each and every time. Today this is not the case, as more and more actors have shifted towards television and film. Today there are a fair number of actors who have never performed in front of a live audience outside of an acting class. This exercise reminds you that the audience is a very important part of the acting equation. Without an audience, to whom will you tell your story?

To understand that acting is a subjective art

What is most fascinating about listening to twenty people talk about the same movie is that you will get twenty different views. One person might walk out looking bored out of her skull while another might leave with a spring to his step and a big smile across his face. A couple might stand up and start kissing after watching a romantic movie. Another couple might leave rather abruptly as the girlfriend realizes her boyfriend does not treat her the way the film's heroine was treated. One guy might turn to his friend and say, "That movie sucked!" Another guy might turn to his wife and say, "That was the best movie I have seen all year!" This reminds us that acting is a subjective art where everyone gets to be an expert. Some actors say they only care about the opinion of their agent or of the head of a studio. But these are not the people who will make you a success. It is the public that decides your ultimate fate based on whether they like what you have to offer. Have a great deal of respect for the audience so that they may return the compliment in kind.

34. In the Footsteps of Legends

For this exercise, rent a silent movie starring a legendary actor, such as Charlie Chaplin, Harold Lloyd, or Buster Keaton. Watch the movie, and when you get to a scene with some really excellent physicality, pause the film. Watch the scene again and then mimic what you have just seen — mimic the physicality of this great legend. To "mimic" is to copy or imitate the actor's physicality; this in itself is not acting.

Perhaps you rented *The Kid* with Charlie Chaplin, and paused at the scene where Chaplin starts to shake his legs in fear. Copy him, and shake your legs the same way. Don't concern yourself too much with finding the meaning behind the actions; rather, copy the physical actions as best you can. The three actors I mentioned above are great comedic actors, so see if you can find the physical humor as you mimic their work.

There is a great deal of physicality in terms of facial expressions, so don't forget to explore this as well. You may pick and choose the moments you want to copy. You might work on five or six different physical actions from different parts of the movie. Don't forget to find the physical humor if it's there. You may have to watch the scene seven or eight times to get the physical action just right. It is not important that you do it well; rather, it is more important that you put in a little time and effort. Don't limit yourself to the actors listed above; there are many great legends to choose from. The only requirements are that the movie is silent, comedic in parts, and that in your opinion the actor is a legend.

Variables:

Rent a speaking movie with one of your favorite actors of all time. Choose certain parts of the movie where he or she has a speech or a phrase that you enjoy. Pause the movie and play that scene again, only this time, close your eyes. Then mimic the actor vocally. In other words, do an impression of the actor. If you like, you can also act out the actor's physicality as you do your vocal impression. Go through different scenes in the movie and repeat this exercise.

Discussion:

In your opinion, what made this actor a legend?

Were you able to copy the physical actions to a satisfactory degree?

Do you think the actor was born with his talent, or did he work hard to develop it?

What are the difficulties of bringing out comedy within physical action?

Purpose:

To emulate the physicality of a legend

If you are going to learn, why not learn with the best? That is perhaps oversimplifying matters, but you get a sense of how the greats did it. Some of the greatest movies ever made are arguably from the silent era. This being said, you cannot ignore the importance of physicality in acting. Not only is it your job to lift the words off the page, it is also your job to allow the words to fly off the page. Engage your entire body in your acting; your body has much to say. Not engaging your body is like getting in a rowboat without oars. It is amazing to watch some of the great actors from yesteryear at work. By getting up and working as they work, it's as if you are right there alongside them. You can sit down and twiddle your thumbs, you can sit by your phone and wait for your agent/manager to call, or you can get up and work this exercise.

To explore the comedy within the action

I asked you to choose a comedy movie because I wanted you to see if you could recreate the humor. To create humor within physical action is not an easy thing to do. When you watch these legends at work, you will see that the comedic timing oozes out of their bodies. How does one recreate this? How does one develop comedic timing? Some people will tell you that you are either born with comedic timing or you are not. Some people will tell you that you are either born to be an actor or not. If you believe that you do not fall into these categories, that is a limiting belief. If, indeed, you are not a "natural talent" (as most of us are not) it simply means you have to be prepared to work that much harder. This activity gives you the opportunity to start working hard right away. There is an art and a science to humor. The science comes in part from the timing and the set of circumstances, and the art comes from within you. In this exercise you get to watch, learn, and explore. Many members of the public love to watch something light and entertaining that makes them laugh and helps take their minds off their day. This means that many of the films and TV shows out there will fit into this category. If you do not work on your physicality and your comedic timing, you are greatly limiting your potential to be cast. As an actor, you need to be as versatile as a piece of soft clay that can be molded in any direction, shape, or form.

35. Music Matters

Pick five very different songs from your music collection. For instance, one song may be very slow and another may be very upbeat. One song might be classical, while another song might be punk rock. At least one or two of these songs should have no words.

Once you have selected your songs, grab a pen and paper. Number your paper one to five, leaving enough space to write a few sentences between each number. Play the first song, close your eyes for the first minute, and simply listen. Upon opening your eyes, write down as many adjectives as you can to describe what you are feeling and imagining in response to the song. Take a moment to digest what is going on inside of you as you listen. Do this for all five songs, remembering to close your eyes for roughly a minute before commencing writing for each one. On one song, you might come up with a large list while another may be only a few words.

Once you have played all five songs, play the first song again at a lower volume and slowly read your list of words for that song over the music. Do this for all five songs. Once you have finished this, digest your discoveries.

Variables:

Perhaps on one occasion you can listen to five songs that have no words and on another they can be five songs that all have words.

Discussion:

How did hearing these songs affect you physically?

Did you find that your thought patterns changed instantaneously from one song to the next?

What happened to your imagination when you were asked to close your eyes during that first minute?

What, in your opinion, is the "power of music?"

Purpose:

Preparation for a performance or audition

Let's assume for a moment you are performing in a play that is based on true romance. You are playing a role that involves romantic scenes. Is it possible that you can play music at home that will enable you to move in this direction? Is it possible that you have romantic music or a song that releases certain feelings in you? How about if you are going for an audition and your confidence is so low that you don't even feel like going? Perhaps you could find songs in your music collection that are able to energize you and build your confidence. A good director knows how to utilize music to affect the audience. As an actor, you can also use music to affect and influence yourself.

To affect and influence the audience

Although this is not an area that you control as an actor, it is important that you are aware of the effects of music on the audience. The right song at the beginning of a movie sets the tone and puts the audience exactly where the director wants them to be. For instance, a fast-paced song may send adrenaline rushing through the audience. It may set them on the edge of their seats, full of anticipation for a fast paced action scene that is to follow. For an example of how powerful music can be, think about your favorite horror movie. What if we took some of that spine-chilling music and exchanged it with something soft and wistful? I think you would find that your favorite horror movie had turned into a comedy. As I have said, even though you will not have any direct influence over the music as an actor, you should be aware of how it can be manipulated to affect the audience. The more elements you are aware of, the more complete picture you have of your craft.

36. Footprints

For this exercise, find some kind of footpath that is covered in snow. If you do not live near snow, you can do this activity equally as well in sand or mud. Make footprints in the snow, but instead of making a straight path, walk in a zigzag or some uncoordinated path. The more illogical your path, the better, provided it is always moving forward. Once you have made your path, move a small distance away and watch to see if people who walk in that direction start to follow your footprints. Make your path a minimum of one hundred yards so you get a good idea of whether people are following your steps or not. Watch a minimum of five people and review your findings. Choose a semi-busy area for this activity; otherwise, you may be waiting all day.

Variables:

See what other types of surfaces you can make footprints on.

Discussion:

How creative did you make your path?
Were you surprised by people's reactions? Explore your findings.
What was the most fascinating part of observing other people?

Purpose:

Exploring human behavior

It is important for the actor to understand why human beings do the things they do. In this exercise you get to observe people and see how they react to your footprints. Even though your footprints follow an illogical path, you will find that a number of people will go along with your path without consideration. This seems an odd behavior, and yet humans will often make choices which seem illogical and unprocessed. Hitler, for example, managed to get millions of people to follow along with his crazy ideas. Even if at first they strongly protested, eventually they blended in to his way of thinking.

Human behavior is so important for the actor to explore because when you play one character after another, it is important to differentiate each one. It is important to make bold choices and understand why your characters do the things they do. Laughter, for instance, causes physiological changes in the body. As Jessica Franke explains, "The surge of happiness that accompanies laughter is caused by stimulation of the dopamine centers in the brain and the release of endorphins, powerful pain-buffering molecules whose actions are mimicked by opiate drugs like morphine."[2] Laughter is not merely a little chuckle; it is a physical and chemically-based phenomenon. Human behavior is quite complex when you think about all of the ingredients that influence it. To study, observe, and begin to understand why people do the things they do is part of your responsibility as an actor.

To utilize a scientific approach to your acting experience

In science there are always hypotheses followed by experiments and results. In this exercise you get to use this approach for your acting discoveries. You can make a hypothesis that sixty percent of people will follow your footprints. By observing, you will be able to discover to what degree this is true. At the end of the exercise, you will have a set of data which you can explore and evaluate. It is not enough to just theorize in acting; it is important to have solid evidence to back up your work. Acting is about being creative and using our imaginations. It is also about pulling and utilizing resources from the real world.

---

[2]Jessica Franke, "Laughter: The Official Medicine of Captain Obvious," *Fibromyalgia Aware* (CA: Lynne Matallana, 2006), 16.

Chapter 7
Voice

37. Vibrations

For this exercise, find an open space and hum the letter M. If you are doing this correctly, it should sound like "Mmmm." Now place the back of your hand on your cheek as you hum. You should be able to feel a vibration through your hand. Once you have accomplished this, place your hand on your forehead and hum again. You'll probably find that you have to hum at a higher pitch in order to feel the vibration in your hand. Next, place your hand on the back of your neck and see if you can feel the vibration. Next, put your hand on your belly and find the vibration. Finally, put your hand on your lower back and see if you can feel the vibration here. This is going to be quite difficult for many people, so be diligent. You may have to hum in a considerably lower octave to actually find the results for this one.

When you're working with different parts of your body, shift your focus to these areas. Adjust your pitch accordingly depending on the area of placement in your body. When you're working with your head, for example, shift your focus to your head; perhaps you will have to hum in a "head voice." The five areas to look at are the cheeks, the forehead, the back of the neck, the belly, and the lower back. If you find there is one area you can't find the vibration for, stay there and experiment for a while. If you still cannot get it, move on and come back to it later.

Variables:

Try and see if you can find vibrations on other parts of your body. How about humming vibrations into your legs?

For another variable, see Exercise 24: Pranayama (page 51).

Discussion:

In which area of your body was it most difficult to find a vibration? How did you manage to solve this?

How much time did you put aside for this activity? Did you give it enough time?

Can you think of any benefits of this activity before reading the "purpose" section?

Purpose

To understand voice placement

In this exercise you are asked to work with different placements of your voice to create different vibrations in your body. When an actor takes on different accents or dialects for a role, he constantly has to work with different placements of his voice. An actor doing a Cockney accent, for example, will most likely have his voice emanating from the throat. This accent often sounds quite rough and forced. A character with a more middle-class upbringing, on the other hand, will have her voice emanating from her diaphragm and even the front of her mouth. Of course I am generalizing on each of these, but nonetheless the placement for each dialect has quite a profound effect on the sound it produces. If you don't understand the vocal placement for a dialect or accent, your accent will always be lacking something.

This not only applies to dialect work, but is equally true for any characterization work you have to do. Being in command of your voice is an important part of your work. As Cicely Berry explains, "I know a great many people worry deeply about how they speak and how they sound, and that this anxiety often stops them expressing themselves as fully as they would wish."[1] It is vital that, as an actor, you are able to express yourself fully in your work. This takes time, patience, and the willingness to train and practice.

Being able to focus your center of attention

In this exercise you are asked to focus your attention in a very specific way. If you are going to find a vibration through your forehead, then you have to focus your attention there. It becomes even more difficult to focus your attention in areas such as your lower back, and yet you must do this in order to accomplish the results. When you are working on a scene, all of your attention must be right there. Even with the camera crew, producer, or gaffer in the background, your attention must stay within your bubble of focus. If, for example, you have to use your imagination to transport yourself to the ocean, your circle of attention may need to grow to a wider circumference, which means your level of concentration will need to be even greater. The benefits of this exercise are numerous when you open yourself up to the possibilities.

---

[1]Cicely Berry, *Your Voice and How to Use It Successfully* (London: Harrap Limited, 1990), 7.

38. Tongue Tipping

For this exercise you are going to need a mouth, preferably your own. Using the tip of your tongue, count every one of your teeth. Start in the upper left corner of your mouth, and when you get all the way to the other side, work right to left on the bottom teeth. This is not a race against time; make sure you touch every single tooth in your mouth with the tip of your tongue. If you are touching more than one tooth at a time, you need to make a more definitive point with your tongue. Repeat this activity five times without stopping.

Variables:

Vary the speed of this exercise so you start slowly and increase the speed with each round. You can also practice kissing which can be an excellent tongue exercise. Kissing is both pleasurable and a wonderful articulation exercise.

Discussion:

Did you find at any point you were counting more than one tooth at any given time? If you answered yes, how did you solve this challenge?

If an activity is quite basic, can it also be extremely beneficial at the same time? Explain your answer.

This activity can be worked virtually any time and any place. Why is practicality an important part of the actor's lifestyle?

Purpose:

To increase your tongue's level of articulation

Some actors are unaware of the significance of the tongue in regards to articulation. Growing up in London, I was told I had a lazy tongue which veered my dialect more towards a London cockney. I was really proud of this fact, but it did not give me the vocal versatility an actor needs. This activity encourages you to pursue articulation of your tongue, which greatly affects the sounds coming out of your mouth. Let's say you are in a film and you are doing an outstanding job, but one fourth of everything you say is lost because of poor articulation. Your audience will become frustrated. Hopefully there is nothing written in the dialog that should not be there. This being said, it is your job to communicate completely to the audience. I am a firm believer in actors using their individuality and utilizing their dialects, but not at the expense of others. You can have a New York accent and still articulate;

you can have a Panamanian accent and still articulate — it is all a matter of practice. When an audience leaves the theatre, they should have been communicated to on a kinesthetic, auditory, and visual level. It is your responsibility as an actor to make sure that this is the case.

To increase your marketability

In this exercise you are taking one more step towards speaking more clearly and simply warming up before a performance. When you are at an audition, you are putting yourself on the line. You are telling the director, "This is what I have to offer." If you do a fine performance but the director has to struggle to understand you, you are unlikely to get a callback. Remember, it is often the producers of the movie who pull the purse strings, and they don't like taking risks. An actor who cannot be understood is a risk because many of today's public are used to comfort and don't like having to make extra effort. For a good example of this, turn your television volume to low so that you have to lean forward to hear what is being said. That extra effort will usually make you lose interest in the scene and possibly the whole movie. Continue to work on your articulation so that you continue to expand your marketability.

39. Dialectician

Today, choose a dialect and spend the whole day speaking with that dialect. Choose a dialect rather than an accent because a dialect is more specific. If you say, "I am going to do an English accent," I would ask you, "Which one?" Let's say you decide on a London dialect, of which there are many. These can be broken up into many different categories such as cockney, middle class, or upper class. Make a specific choice. If you choose a Texan dialect, consider whether you are looking at East Texas, Central Texas, or South Texas, to name a few. There is no such thing as a general American accent any more than there is a general British accent. Once you have chosen your specific dialect, you are almost ready to begin.

Before you begin, do some background research on your dialect. Research the region you have chosen. Books, documentaries, and the Internet will all be great resources. Additionally, research how the dialect came about. See what you can find out about what makes a cockney a cockney. Was cockney formed originally from other dialects? How and why does the use of hands play into the cockney dialect?

Cockneys are considered to be very proud Londoners; how does this play into your dialect interpretation? Find out about the city of London, the history of London, how Londoners live, and what Londoners do for fun. You are doing this research in order to become more intimate with the dialect you have chosen. If, once you begin this exercise, you sound even remotely the way you should, people will probably ask you where you are from. Someone will almost definitely ask you questions about your country or city, and it would be really interesting if you were actually able to answer them accurately. The more you understand your dialect, the more you will believe in the authenticity in what you are doing. A dialect is not spoken just from the neck up, but also affects the way you move, stand, walk, and express yourself with or without your hands. You may want to do your research on one day and go out and use your dialect on another.

On the day you use your dialect, spend the whole day doing whatever you need to do. The only exception is that you are going to use your dialect the whole day. Try to do this on a day when you are not going to be around too many people who know you, as this may cause a conflict of interest. If you are in the bookstore, the grocery store, the bank, the coffee shop, or wherever else you go, you will use your dialect. Some people may not even bat an eyelid, while others may look at you a second or two longer. Some people may strike up a conversation while others will not. Be prepared for a variety of questions that relate to your dialect. The only given rule for this exercise is that you stay in your dialect for the entire day. When you get home, review your findings.

Variables:

If you are feeling somewhat shy there are a few ways you can counter this. One option is to spend your day on the phone using your dialect. For instance you could phone up a music store and ask them if they have a specific CD in stock. This is actually a bigger challenge because when a person cannot see you, their sense of hearing will become heightened. If you don't want to go on your own, take a friend with you who is going to use a different dialect. Be careful here that you do not spend the day laughing at each other. If you are going to go together, make sure that you agree beforehand to take the exercise seriously.

For other variables, see Exercise 49: Physical Expressions (page 102) and Exercise 84: *Aprender Idioma* (page 172).

Discussion:

Were you surprised by people's reactions?

How challenging was it to keep the dialect going all day?

Were you able to answer questions convincingly when asked about your country or city of origin?

How does a well-done dialect help define a character?

Purpose:

To expand your character range

In the professional world you are going to be typecast. You may not like this, but it is a fact of the business side of acting. If you can work with dialects convincingly, you have just expanded your character range. Let's say you are always cast as "the best friend." If you are from New York and can also do an amazing middle-class London dialect, you have an expanded character range. You can now be cast as "the best friend" in English-based movies as well as American-based films. Perhaps you are a theatre student and your school is performing *Romeo and Juliet*. While this play can be done quite successfully with American dialects, the director of this particular production is asking for English dialects at the audition. If you have been practicing these dialects, you are going to have the edge on some of the other actors who haven't practiced. Consider carefully which dialects you take the time and effort to learn. There are some dialects that you will never use and therefore are only useful for personal gratification. Similarly, it is better to have two impeccable dialects that you can work with than five that you are only okay with.

To understand the importance of research

If you are able to do an excellent cockney dialect but do not understand that cockneys are very expressive and almost always talk with their hands, you will only have mastered half a dialect. You will sound right, but your body will contradict your voice. If you were in London, people might not say anything, but there would be an odd quality to you that didn't quite fit. If you were in London and you had not done any research on the city, you would probably not be able to answer any question convincingly. This does not mean you could not do a convincing accent; it simply means you would not be convincing in your dialect. I do not expect one day of research to teach you everything you need to know. If you are planning on working with your chosen dialect over many years, then continue your research over an extended period of time. Perhaps one year you can take a trip to London and learn firsthand about the culture and the people. I want you to think of a dialect in the same way you would think about learning a new language. Cicely Berry, a world-renowned voice instructor, explains, "It seems to me that words are the most primitive and the most sophisticated things we possess. They started out as primitive sounds to express needs of survival and have developed into a most advanced means of communication."[2] It is the actor's job to communicate a story by whatever means he has available. You do not stop learning new words, but continue to expand your vocabulary over time.

40. Less Is More/More Is Less

Learn the following dialog and become familiar with it: "It is not your right to tell us how we should live. It is not your place to stand here before us and make the speeches that you make. It is for each of us to find our own way, and nothing you say will change that — nothing." Feel this dialog out for a few minutes and make some assumptions: Who is talking? Where is the scene taking place? To whom is the character talking? What is the conflict? What does the character want?

Perform the scene in a quiet whisper. Work the scene as if these words are only meant to be heard by one person immediately within your close proximity. Who is this individual? Why is he the only person you are telling this to? Perhaps this element will totally change the way you interpret the scene.

Now perform the scene, adjusting your projection to reach a group of about four or five people gathered around you. Perhaps you are at a meeting in the factory where you work and you are addressing one of your superiors. Perhaps at the end of the meeting you get fired for the way you have spoken to your boss; however, you keep your sense of dignity. As you adjust your volume, make sure it is just right to address the four or five people gathered around — no more, no less.

Perform the scene again, this time using enough projection to address the entire room. Imagine that you are talking to one hundred people. What is the scene now? Perhaps there is an entirely different storyline developing from the one you originally had. Make sure your projection is just right for the space and amount of people you need to reach.

[2]Berry, 40.

Work this exercise one final time. This time, project as if you are addressing ten thousand people. Look at the dialog and decide why this topic might be discussed with all these people. Perhaps it is some sort of political rally related to addressing a former dictator. How will your projection reach ten thousand people? Why are ten thousand people listening to you? This projection should sound quite different from when you addressed the individual at the start of this exercise. Really work to enhance your sense of believability here to reach all these individuals.

Variables:

Watch a movie, adjusting the volume at different stages. How does this affect the movie for you? Does it affect the way you receive the movie?

Discussion:

What is the importance of sometimes using your voice in an intimate setting?

When might you need to use your voice in softer overtones?

What is the importance of being aware of your projection and knowing how to manipulate it?

If you are involved in the film industry, do you think it is still necessary to command your own voice?

Purpose:

To adapt your projection to any performance space

Let's assume that you're an actor who was raised in the theatre and you've also been to college for your acting training. You know better than anyone how important projection is. You have now switched your interests to film and television. Today you are auditioning for an agent, and you are going to do a monolog. You remember that you want every word to be heard and understood, so you use a booming voice that vibrates around the room. Unfortunately, you are in a tiny office performing for this poor individual who is sitting two feet in front of you. If your volume is overbearing, he will not hear your piece, just your incredibly irritating voice. This is a complaint that agents make time and time again. You must understand how to adapt to your environment, whatever that may be. You also might come in for an audition where you were planning to start the piece off very strong only to discover that the reader is very soft spoken, so you decide to adapt to a different interpretation. If you do this, you have to have the vocal technique to understand how to do it successfully. It is imperative that you adjust your volume to your space and your environment. Perhaps you are in a crowd scene where there are supposed to be about one hundred people milling around. You are having a heart to heart with your son, attempting to talk some good into him. What you have to say is for his ears and his only. If this scene were for television, you could practically whisper it and the mike would pick everything up. If this were for theatre, however, you would have to work with a projected form of a whisper that would sound totally different. Not only do you need versatility in your projection, you need to understand voice and how and when to use it.

To create tenderness and volatility when needed

Being able to manipulate your vocal levels will allow you more versatility in your acting. Perhaps in a particular scene you are being flirtatious with a young man whom your character wants as a future boyfriend. You inflect soft undertones in your voice to come across as sexy and alluring. Perhaps on another project you are playing a part where danger, stubbornness, and lack of self control are the order of the day. Manipulation of your voice and projection levels is not a substitution for other aspects of your acting; rather it is another vital piece of the acting equation. Some people also assume that in television and film they will never need to project. This is not the case — sometimes you might have to use your projection for the same scene twenty times in a row. This exercise shows how by changing your vocal levels you can totally change the meaning of the piece. This is powerful and necessary information for the actor to have.

Chapter 8
Sensory Awareness

41. Night Vision

The following activity might make you feel like you are physically stepping out of your comfort zone. This is good; as an actor you have to step outside of your comfort zone on a constant basis. Cover your eyes with something such as a scarf, a bandanna, or anything that leaves you in a world of darkness. If you don't want to cover your eyes, you can simply close them provided you are able to do so for a prolonged period of time. Spend a minimum of one hour without your vision. Don't simply sit down and wait for your hour to be over; keep busy completing activities and tasks. Perhaps you can go into your kitchen and wash the dishes, make your bed, take a shower, or vacuum the floor. How about making and eating your lunch? Before you start this exercise, set your alarm so that you know exactly when your time is up. When you open your eyes after the exercise, take a moment to process everything you have just been through. Many actors comment on how profound this experience is. Rather than just talking about it, I'd rather have you experience it.

Variables:

Wear earplugs for at least one hour. Try watching television, listening to music, and having a conversation with friends. Because you are not used to losing your sense of hearing or sight, I encourage you to work these exercises in a controlled space such as your home.

Discussion:

What was the first thing you noticed when you lost your sense of sight?

What was the most difficult task for you to complete and why?

What happened to your other senses when you lost your sense of sight?

What was the most important discovery you made during this activity?

At any time did you experience an element of fear during this activity?

Purpose:

To enhance the use of your different senses

When you lose the use of one sense, you will find that your other senses become sharpened and stronger. Many actors comment that their sense of touch becomes much more apparent during this exercise. They are able to touch a blanket and really feel its depth and softness, or wipe a surface and discover its texture. It is one thing to theorize about acting and another thing to experience it. If you are on a studio set and you have to give the impression that you are on a beautiful golden beach, how are you going to do that? I'm sure the heat from the lights will help you, but what about the sound of the ocean and the crashing of the waves? How about the smell of the saltwater? As Uta Hagen comments, "Full human contact employs all the senses, the more intense they are, the more highly they are developed, the more available is potential of the actor — his talent."[1] The more you are able to sharpen and use your senses, the easier it will be to take maximum advantage of them.

To encourage the actor to take risks

When you take away your sense of sight, there is a potential for you to bump into a cupboard or a door. While I hope this does not happen to you, you are taking a physical risk. You are putting trust in yourself that you will be able to complete a task of your choosing. If you choose to make your breakfast and are unable to do so, this may become a humbling experience for you, and so you are taking a risk. In this exercise, if you fail to complete your task or literally fall flat on your face, I hope you realize that it is the journey of the discovery, and not necessarily the end result, that is important. Too often an actor will hold back during a rehearsal or during a performance because he does not want to look stupid or embarrass himself. In holding back, he achieves the very thing he was hoping to avoid. His work looks awkward and unexplored as he fails to live on the edge of his character. I'm not talking about starting a fight in a rehearsal because it goes with your character — this would not be acting. I'm talking about committing to each and every scene one hundred percent even if that means making mistakes. Yogi Berra once said he only had to strike out seventy percent of the time. If you are willing to strike out sometimes, perhaps you, too, can make the hall of fame.

---

[1]Uta Hagen, *Respect for Acting* (New York: Macmillan Publishing Company, 1973), 60.

42. Seeing Is Believing

Find yourself a comfortable chair. Look down at the floor or close your eyes to prepare yourself, and when you look up, visualize the ocean right before your eyes. Don't move around or use your body or facial muscles to signify anything. The only part of your body you are allowed to move in any way is your eyes. In other words, you are going to have to portray being on the beach with only the use of your eyes to tell the story. Actually, you have many more resources available to create this scene. Use your imagination to see the ocean, smell the saltwater and seaweed, feel the sand between your toes and the warmth of the sun against your skin, hear the sound of crashing waves and the seagulls flying above, and taste the saltwater as it sprays across your face and causes your throat to become partially dry. Do all of this while sitting in a chair and using only your eyes. When you have explored the ocean scenario, come up with another, such as the inside of a church, a forest, a snow-capped mountain, or a football match. Remember, you are not miming a scene, but simply using your eyes and utilizing your senses and imagination to their full capacity.

When I've used this exercise in group situations, the audience is asked to guess where the actor is. As you are working individually, you will not get that feedback. You've heard the saying, "Be your own biggest fan and your own toughest critic." At this point, be your own toughest critic. Don't let anything slide; if you are not happy with your performance then explore until you are. Just a little reminder: these activities can be utilized again and again. It is a bit like going to the gym — you don't say, "I went one time so I am done"; you keep going back.

Variable:

Try this activity without using your senses (except sight) in any way. Note what the differences are from the previous assignment.

Discussion:

How long did you spend on this activity? Do you think that was enough time?

When are you going to utilize this activity again?

Did you find it became more realistic for you when you utilized your senses?

What were the challenges of only being able to use your eyes?

Purpose:

To be able to work in different mediums such as TV and film

In this exercise you had to get all of the information across simply with the use of your eyes. In TV and film you are going to find that this skill will serve you well. Let's say you are a theatre-trained actor and are used to physicalzing a great deal. You have found that this is of great importance for stage work, but you've recently been cast in a TV show with lots of close-ups. The director wants you to tell the story with your eyes and facial expressions, and you find this a challenge because you're not used to such a subtle approach. Get used to it, and get used to it fast! As an actor, if you want to work you are going to have to be versatile and be able to mold yourself in any direction needed. Acting is acting, but the technical aspects of film are quite different from those of the stage. All I ask is that you become a master of both.

To understand and utilize your senses

If you are going to convince one person in this exercise, convince yourself. If you do not believe you are looking at the ocean, neither will we. In this activity I ask you to use your senses, and by doing so you are training them and heightening their capabilities and awareness. Just as a tree that survives a hurricane builds stronger roots, I want you to build strong roots with your acting. Working with your senses on one occasion is fine, but it will not build strong roots. Some actors will tell me that they will do these things once they have a script in hand. If you cannot do them at a base level, what makes you think you will be able to find these moments when the complexities of a script are added? Many people can do a mediocre job in their acting, but we are not interested in those people; we are looking for actors whose work has substance and value and enough versatility to go in any direction they choose.

43. Phone Book Finesse

For this exercise you need a phone book and a hair. Yes, you read correctly — you need a hair. It can be your hair or the hair of a dear friend as long as you have one strand of hair. Place this hair under the first page of your phone book. With your eyes closed, run your fingers over the first page and see if you can stop your fingers over the hair. Basically, try to feel the hair through the page. Use your fingertips as opposed to your whole hand. Once you have successfully completed this, put the hair beneath two pages, three pages, four pages, and so on.

See how many pages you can get through and still feel the hair with your fingers. There is no rush to complete this activity. Perhaps you'll get to ten pages on the first day and fifteen pages on another occasion. For the purpose of this activity, it is important that you close your eyes so that you can only rely on your sense of touch to guide you. Closing your eyes will heighten your sense of touch to its maximum potential. Once you have finished the exercise, you may discard the hair unless you wish to keep it for sentimental reasons.

Variables:

Instead of using a human hair try working with your pet's hair. A cat's hair would probably be quite a challenge as it is usually thinner than human hair.

Discussion:

Did you find that closing your eyes heightened your sense of awareness?

Would this activity be easier or more difficult using a magazine?

When this activity became more difficult, did you give up or did you find a way to continue?

What surprised you most about this activity?

Purpose:

To develop your sense of touch

In this exercise you are enabling your sense of touch to become heightened and more sensitive. To feel a strand of hair through the pages of a phone book can take an enormous amount of sensitivity through the fingertips. The more you practice, the greater amount of sensitivity to touch you will have. Having a skill such as this can be invaluable to the actor. Let's say you are playing a romantic scene in a film and the director asks you to lightly caress your partner's cheek with the back of your hand. If you do not possess the skill of finesse, your caress may feel abrasive. This may set the wrong atmosphere for the scene and cause your partner to become frustrated and even aggravated. The greater degree of understanding you have of your sense of touch, the more flexibility it will give you in your work.

To improve concentration and focus

If you do not focus on the task at hand, you will not succeed in this exercise. This may seem like a strange statement since you will still be able to feel the hair through a number of pages. The challenge is that you will never be able to reach your true potential. Sometime when you watch a movie you will say to yourself, "That actor did a pretty good job." If you think about this statement for a minute, you will realize that what you are saying is that the actor could have done better. Without concentration in your acting — whether during the performance itself or in the preparation stages — something will always be lacking. By utilizing an activity such as this one over a continual period of time, you have the opportunity to make concentration and focus an automatic process for you.

44. Sense of Smell

Raid your house and come up with seven distinct-smelling items. Some examples are a piece of cedar wood, a rosebud, an unwashed T-shirt, a cup of herbal tea, a bottle of cologne, and an old book. Take your seven items and find someplace comfortable to sit, or, if you prefer, you can find someplace uncomfortable to sit. Close your eyes and spend a good minute smelling each item. When you are finished with each item, open your eyes and write down all the feelings, sensations, and memories going through your mind and body. Let's say you smelled a piece of cedar wood for one minute. You might say the cedar made you feel calm, relaxed, content, nostalgic, and peaceful. It may trigger a memory of walking out in a beautiful forest on an autumn day. Whatever comes to mind or body, write it down. Once you have finished with one item, move on to the second one. You may want to have a little jar of coffee beans handy to help neutralize your sense of smell between items. This will allow you to move on to each separate item without the smells from the previous item lingering in your nose.

Variables:

Spend a week or two with this exercise. Take an item such as a bottle of cologne and, when you are having the most amazing day, smell the cologne and write down everything that comes to mind. Set the bottle aside and, when you are having an absolutely depressing day, pick the bottle up, smell it again, and write down everything that comes to mind. Do this over the period of one or two weeks, utilizing at least three separate emotional experiences. Do emotions have the ability to affect and change our sense of smell?

Discussion:

What item impacted you the most?

Were you surprised by your reactions to any of the items you smelled?

How does our sense of smell play a role in acting?

How can smells be used to enhance the experience for a live theatre audience?

Purpose:

To raise the importance of the sense of smell

In this exercise you are asked to smell a number of items. As you smell each item you may find that it causes a physical reaction in your body that triggers one or more memories. If this is the case, then it is important information to have. It means that there is another method of influencing your reactions, interpretations, and experiences. Of all the senses, I would harbor a guess that the sense of smell is the one least utilized and explored. If we can create such strong and diverse reactions and experiences simply through our sense of smell, then shouldn't it be manipulated and utilized more fully?

To enhance the audience's experience

Imagine going to a play or a movie where they incorporated the sense of smell. As you were watching the beach scene, they sent a mild infusion of saltwater and seaweed through the air. As you were watching the scene in the field, an infusion of honeysuckle and daisies drifts past your nose. The result of such actions may increase the potential for the audience to be transported to the place they are viewing. The logistics and practicality of this idea are one thing, but what I am interested in is the concept. Anything that enhances our theatre-going experience needs to be developed and explored. As an actor, the more senses you can involve, the more your imagination can be unleashed.

45. Step by Step

For this exercise, go to a park, a nature reserve, or anywhere you can clearly hear people walking. Start walking, and as a person walks behind you, make certain assumptions based on the sound of that person's walk. All you have to go on is the sound of the person's footsteps. Decide what the person looks like. How tall is the person? What is the person's physical weight? Is the person attractive or plain? What hair color does the person have? What eye color does the person have? Is the person male or female? What does the person do for a living?

Listen to the speed at which the person is walking and make additional assumptions based on this. What type of personality does the person have? Does the person live with a lot of stress, or is the person more laid back? How is the person feeling at this exact moment? What is the person thinking about at this exact moment? Make these judgments in a very short period of time. You may only have ten to fifteen seconds before this individual overtakes you. Once the person passes you, decide how much of your original assumptions were accurate. If you picked male and the person happens to be a female, you know that this is one area you misinterpreted. You do not have to write anything down for this exercise. Try to work this exercise on five or ten different people.

Variables:

Instead of listening to footsteps, you could listen to a person talking behind you and make the same assumptions as before. This is going to be a little easier, and most likely you will already know the person's gender.

Discussion:

What was the most compelling part of listening to footsteps?

How did you make so many assumptions in such a short period of time?

What is the most fascinating part of this exercise?

How can you improve on this activity?

Purpose:

To become sensory aware

In this exercise, all you have to go on is the sound of an individual's footsteps. The only sense you can utilize fully is your sense of hearing. It is also possible to engage your sense of smell if the person is wearing after-shave or perfume or if they haven't washed in a while. Not only is it interesting to base all this information on your sense of hearing, but what is even more fascinating is if some of it actually turns out to be correct. Your physical assumptions would become immediately clear as soon as you saw the person. If you thought he was male and six feet tall, you would be able to tell if you were correct straight away. It is more difficult to know if your personal assumptions are correct; however, you will have some idea. If you said he sounded like a stressed individual and he passed you with a frown on his face and a wrinkled forehead, you may have been on the right track. As an actor, not only do you want to utilize your senses on an ongoing basis, but you also want to appreciate their value. An actor who does not utilize his senses will limit his acting potential.

For fun

As you get to make all these assumptions about someone you have not even seen, it can be rather fun to discover that some of your assumptions are actually correct. It is great that as an actor you want people to take you seriously. I would like to suggest, however, that you do not take yourself too seriously. If everything about your acting is serious with no room to maneuver, where is the fun in that? *The American College Dictionary* defines fun as, "A source of enjoyment."[2] Allow your acting and career to be a source of enjoyment and discovery in your life. Remember, when you started your acting journey, you probably did so because you decided it was fun. Never allow the fun side to leave you because it is this side that will keep you going when the going gets tough. Directors and agents hear all the time, "I want to be taken seriously." This is a cliché line in the industry. Be professional and come as a breath of fresh air to all that you do.

46. Audience Appreciation

Set aside your role as an actor for this exercise and become a member of the audience. Put a movie on and, as you are watching it, play with the volume. As you turn the volume up and down, pay attention to how this affects your enjoyment of the performance. When you are at a movie theatre, notice if the volume is too loud or too quiet and how this affects you. What if you are at a play and you cannot hear what the actors are saying?

Continue watching your movie and go sit in different parts of your living room. What happens when you sit closer, further away, or to the

[2]David Jost, *The American College Dictionary* (New York: Houghton Mifflin Company, 1997), 551.

far left or right of the room? How does this affect the performance for you? Each time you go to a movie theatre or play, change your seat placement and see how it affects you.

As you watch your movie, play with the lighting in your room. Go from bright lights to no lights, to using a colored light bulb (red, green, blue, etc.). As you are sitting in a movie theatre or play, what happens to you when they turn the lights down? Does this affect or change your behavior in any way?

Now eat some crunchy food as you watch your movie at home. What happens when the guy sitting next to you at the theatre is munching on popcorn or opening candy wrappers? How does this affect your enjoyment of the performance?

How about all the commercials and previews that come on before the movie begins — does this affect you in any way? If you are at a play and someone comes out and talks for fifteen minutes about why the play was written, etc., is this useful or detrimental in your opinion?

When you are finished, review your findings.

Variables:

I have given you a few areas I want you to play with to see how elements outside the performance affect the actual performance. See if you can come up with other elements that affect how you watch a performance or movie.

Discussion:

Which element that you changed had the most profound effect on you?

How important are these elements in your enjoyment of the movie or performance?

In what ways should an audience's awareness needs be addressed?

How important is the audience to the actor?

Purpose:

**To be aware of the different elements that
influence the audience's experience**

Sometimes it's easy to forget that there are many elements that can affect a person's perception of a performance. Let's say you are at the movies and the person next to you is talking and munching her popcorn in your ear. You might leave and say you didn't enjoy the movie when in fact it was the experience you didn't enjoy. I have sat through a movie where the volume was so loud I could hardly hear myself think, and it affected my enjoyment of the picture as a whole. We have become more impatient as a society and, therefore, we don't like our time to be wasted. Think about how commercials affect the way we watch movies. Although you do not have specific control over some of these elements, it is important that as an actor you are aware that the audience is influenced by many elements outside of the performance itself. This exercise encourages you not to forget the overall experience of an audience member. As an actor you want your work to be recognized, so it is important to be aware of the different elements that can affect this outcome. In this exercise I have purposely not mentioned anything about the movie or performance itself. Every element that affects the performance is part of the performance. I understand that many of these are personally out of your control; I simply want you to be aware of them.

To respect your audience

Sometimes it's easy as an actor to forget that there is an audience or that the audience actually exists. This is especially true for those of you working in television and film, despite the fact that there can potentially be an enormous audience present in regard to the crew and background actors. It is important never to forget the audience because who else are you performing for? Unless you are performing in a vacuum, you are performing with the understanding that your work will be viewed by others. It is important for you, as an actor, to have a deep respect for your audience because they are the ones who will ultimately judge your work. Your acting instructor may say one thing, your best friend another, but the audience will have the final say. To have a deep respect for your audience reminds you that they are in fact part of the acting equation. As David Wood and Janet Grant observe, "If it is a comedy, the amount of laughter will be a good guide, but in a straight play the audience will remain passive and quiet whether or not they are responding with pleasure."[3] This does not mean that during a performance you should change your actions to make your audience laugh more. It means that at the back of your mind you must remember that you are telling a story, and you want to get your message across to those who want to hear it.

[3]David Wood and Janet Grant, *Theatre for Children* (London: Faber and Faber Limited, 1997), 208.

Chapter 9
Body Awareness

47. Sleep Mania

"Are you sitting comfortably? Then I will begin." When I was a small child growing up in London, my mum use to have us listen to stories to send us to sleep. She would always begin her stories in this manner. The reason I mention this is because the first part of this exercise is for you to fall asleep. When you wake up in the morning, this is where your journey really begins. Don't simply get out of bed and get on with your day. Give yourself an extra amount of time in bed to complete this exercise — anywhere between five and fifteen minutes should suffice. Lie in bed and make a mental note of the first thing that goes through your mind. What is the second thing to go through your mind? Do you automatically open your eyes or are there different steps and processes you go through to get to this point? It may take a number of minutes for you to actually open your eyes. Perhaps you lie there for some time with your eyes closed. How do your eyes adjust to the light? Does this take a number of attempts? What part of your body moves first? Do you turn to your left or your right? Do your muscles feel relaxed or tense? Is there a tingling sensation in your feet? Once you have completed this exercise you will never view waking up and getting out of bed the same way again.

Variables:

Reverse the process. Instead of observing yourself waking up, observe yourself falling asleep. I am going to leave the explanation at that. Get used to the idea of being able to do the work with as little direction as possible. Get used to the idea of processing information on your own terms.

Discussion:

What time did you wake up on this particular day? Is this your normal time for waking up?

Think about all the different stages you had to go through in order to wake up. What relevance does that have for your acting?

When you woke up, did you feel like you had been in a deep stage of sleep or a lighter stage of sleep?

Purpose:

To understand detail

When you wake up in the morning, you don't simply get out of bed. Even if you think that is what you do, there is a process that your body goes through in waking up no matter how fleeting or lengthy it may be. In this exercise you get to analyze these stages as you are experiencing them, which can be quite profound. How many times have you seen a movie where the actor is supposedly waking up and you don't buy it? You don't buy it because neither does the actor. A few moments before the scene, the makeup artist was powdering her nose, the cameras were shining light in her eyes, and the director was shouting instructions. Through all of this she has to create that moment of waking up in addition to remembering her lines. This activity will give you a pure form of paying attention to your mind and body as it is going through the process of waking.

You can apply this type of activity to many areas of your life wherever you see fit. One very important message is that you can learn acting and apply it anywhere. While I am an enormous proponent of training through schools, workshops, and productive courses, I want you to realize that you are not limited to these. Your life and the world around you is your training ground should you choose to see it that way.

Experiencing the process one step at a time

This exercise encourages you to experience the process of waking up one step at a time. It allows you to break this process down into specific detail. It may be interesting to note how many different steps you actually go through to wake up fully. If you are cast in a play or movie, then there are certain steps that you will want to take in preparation. Perhaps you will start with reading the script and letting the material sink in. Perhaps you will pick up the play again, reread it, and see if you discover something different this time. Let the lines work on you before you commence working on them. At this juncture you might choose to start learning your lines either as a technical exercise or as a means of searching for intent in the words. By understanding that there are steps that need to be taken, an actor can put more clarity into his work instead of creating a blurred vision.

48. Cry Me a River

Watch a movie that, for you, has always been a real tearjerker. Go through the movie and find the climactic scene, the one that always brings a tear to your eye or makes you break out in full-fledged sobs. As you watch that scene of the movie and start to cry, see if you can pinpoint when exactly the tears started. What was the trigger for the first tear? Analyze what type of tears you are experiencing. Sometimes we experience tears of joy, anger, resentment, fear, and so on. I want you to know specifically what type of tears are flowing.

Stop the movie and take a few minutes to do something totally different. Perhaps you can go in the kitchen and make a cup of herbal tea or polish the mirror in the bathroom. When you come back, start the movie from the same place and see if you get similar results. Do as you did before and pay close attention to what different processes you go through during this activity. Perhaps there is a certain moment in the movie that sends a signal to your heart that causes a sort of crescendo effect and leads you to feel for the characters and triggers tears to well up in your eyes. You are not being asked to invent or force tears or pretend to cry. If nothing happens, so be it. Go find a different movie with similar effects and repeat the exercise. See if things change.

Variables:

Instead of using crying as your prerequisite, look for a scene in a movie that makes you laugh, makes you feel angry, or puts fear into your heart. Again, pay attention to what is happening as it is happening and see if you can record the processes you are going through.

Discussion:

How did you know that the movie would work for you?

How long did it take for the tears to well up in your eyes from the moment you first started the movie?

Were you surprised by the first trigger that got the tears in your eyes?

What happened when you tried it a second time? How did your results differ?

Purpose:

To appreciate the complexities of crying

It seems that there is a myth in the acting world that once you can cry on cue you are an accomplished actor. I have seen many actors who can cry externally on cue to a degree that is so forced it looks ridiculous. In this exercise you are not being asked to cry on cue; rather, you are being asked to find a scene that moves you to tears regardless of your efforts. In this respect there is a big difference in the outcomes and results. An actor who can externally cry on cue might get an audience to give him a round of applause, but an actor who can move an audience to tears may leave them in absolute silence. The purpose of this exercise is not to make yourself cry, but rather to discover the automatic processes that lead you to tears.

To utilize simplistic approaches

This activity is so simplistic that it is almost laughable. You don't do anything; you simply allow yourself to be drawn in to whatever you are watching, and the results automatically follow. It is very powerful to have these tears triggered by an automatic response over which you have no control. It can be quite a profound experience to see this happen in a matter of seconds or minutes. You have not been asked to take any time aside to prepare or to get into character. The only requirement is that you watch the movie. There are many processes and experiences an actor will go through during training, and this is not supposed to replace any of them. Rather, this is supposed to give you a different perspective. I have always liked the fact that this activity is so simplistic, and yet the results can be fascinating.

49. Physical Expressions

Take on a physical expression that is different from your own for an entire day. For instance, you could affect a limp in one leg so that as you put pressure down on one foot it starts to slightly give way. If you choose this expression, then it is going to affect the knee, the ankle, and the hip as you walk. Taking on a limp will also affect the upper body and will be felt in areas such as your shoulders and neck muscles. You might want to take on a lisp with a lazy tongue that is lingering a moment longer than necessary in between the teeth. You will find that this creates a slight speech impediment that affects your vowels, consonants, and pronunciation of words. You could choose to affect a squint in one eye so that the eye muscles become contracted. This eye should then appear to be partially closed. It may be simpler and less of a strain to simply keep one eye closed. Make sure that whatever you choose is not putting too much stress on your body. If this is the case, then switch to a different body part or shorten the length of time you perform the task. It is important that if you choose a limp, for instance, you commit to it in its entirety. Open a door with a limp, go shopping with a limp, sit at the dinner table aware of your limp, and in all other aspects of the day implement this limp. Do not revert to your regular physicality when something is challenging such as walking up a hill; rather, see how you can adapt to the situation. Make observations throughout the day of how your circumstances have changed due to the new set of physical challenges that you are facing.

Variables:

You could take on a different accent or dialect for the day. See Exercise 39: Dialectician (page 80) for more details.

Discussion:

What were the biggest differences in your day with your newly found physical challenges?

In what ways did you find that people responded to you differently?

What was your reason for choosing the particular body part you focused on?

What was the most profound discovery you made during this exercise?

Purpose:

To develop a physical awareness for character work

No two people move, look, or sound exactly the same. This holds true for all the characters that you are going to play throughout your life. This activity allows you to become very familiar with a new physical environment that deeply contrasts your own. The reason I have chosen something that is physically challenging is that the results can be quite profound. As an actor you want to know where your character's center of gravity lies. Some people move with their chest thrust forward, others with their head and neck jutting out, and some people walk with their shoulders leading. You are going to find that through the physical explorations of characters you will make new discoveries about who they really are. There are a number of actors who you can see on any given day who are very successful at playing themselves. A studio often brings them on precisely because they want the actor to play himself or herself, hoping this will translate into a box office success. If this is the type of acting you are searching for, then perhaps this exercise is not as beneficial for you. If, on the other hand, you are looking to define each and every character fully, journey onward.

To make the connection between the physical and chemical

If you stand up and start to jump around with your arms in the air, you are going to find that your body starts to release adrenaline and possibly endorphins as well. If you sit in a chair, cross your legs, fold your arms, and droop your head forward towards your legs you are going to find that your body reacts quite differently, possibly releasing lactic acids. These chemical responses in your body can make quite a difference in a person's life. When you apply physicality to a character and find that this changes your chemical releases throughout your body, you are probably going to find that this in turn affects the personality of your character. Jonnie Patricia Mobley gives a definition of Biomechanics that fits into this category: "A theory of early twentieth century Russian director Vsevolod Meyerhold that actors can use certain patterns of muscular activity to elicit a particular emotion; for example to express joy the actor could turn a somersault."[1]

50. Taste Buds

For this exercise, raid the fridge or pantry and get a piece of bread. Take a moment to look at that piece of bread. Think of exactly how that piece of bread tastes. Once you remember how it tastes, totally forget how it tastes. You are about to transfer a totally different taste onto that piece of bread.

Hold the piece of bread in your hands and close your eyes. Imagine a piece of food you absolutely adore (other than bread). For the moment, let's imagine that it is a piece of dark chocolate cake. Imagine yourself biting into that mouthwatering, delicious, rich, creamy, scrumptious, chocolate cake. Imagine that as you take your first bite into that tender, soft layer, it melts on your tongue. A warm feeling of satisfaction spreads throughout your belly. When your craving and enjoyment for this food is peaked, bite into that piece of bread (with your eyes still closed) as if it is the piece of chocolate cake. Relish, enjoy, and devour that piece of bread just like it was your chocolate cake. See if you have the same sensations going through your body as you did a moment ago when you

---

[1]Jonnie Patricia Mobley, *NTC's Dictionary of Theatre and Drama Terms* (Lincolnwood, IL: National Textbook Company, 1995), 15.

were simply imagining your chocolate cake.

Now open your eyes, stand up, and shake your body loose. Go back to your chair with a new piece of bread. Close your eyes again and this time imagine a piece of food you absolutely detest (again, other than bread). Perhaps you could work with the idea that you are biting into an onion. Go through the same process as above, except this time with all the negative feelings that this food brings to your taste buds. Once you have completed the exercise, open your eyes and review your findings. Stand up and shake everything out before moving on with the rest of your day.

Variables:

Once you feel comfortable in this activity, do it with your eyes open. You can also work with a glass of water, imagining drinks that you enjoy and detest. For another variable, see Exercise 58: Taste Buds 2 (page 118).

Discussion:

Were you able to transfer the actual tastes of the foods you chose to your piece of bread?

What was the most challenging part of this exercise?

Have your feelings towards your piece of bread changed in anyway?

Why should an actor explore the concept of transference?

Purpose:
To utilize the art of transference

In this exercise you are asked to take a plain piece of bread and allow it to become something totally different to your taste buds. This exercise has many implications for you as an actor, but for now let me just touch on one. Let's assume you are working on a restaurant scene in which you are supposedly dining at a very expensive restaurant. Your character is supposed to be eating some Beluga Caviar. Because this food costs thousands of dollars, your director decides to use crushed blackberries instead. As an actor, it is your job to make sure that it appears as if you are eating caviar. Not only in terms of its taste but also in terms of how you put it in your mouth, savor the caviar, and eventually swallow and digest it. You may find yourself in a scene where you are supposed to be drinking fine French sparkling champagne and instead you are given sparkling apple juice. Sometimes a director will use a food substitute because it is simpler and less messy in the mouth.

Perhaps you're in a scene where you need to be eating and talking at the same time. Food transference is going to come up throughout your career as an actor, so this is a very good exercise for you.

To create physiological changes in the body

If you can take a piece of plain bread and make it taste like the most incredible piece of chocolate cake you have ever eaten, you have really accomplished something. If you are able to release endorphins/lactic acids in your body while you bite into this piece of bread, then you have changed your body at a physiological and cellular level. If you are able to alter the response of your taste buds by utilizing your imagination, this is quite an achievement. The physical body cannot be ignored by actors, for it is part of who we are. As Moni Yakim explains, "Most techniques deal with the emotional life of a character but never deal with how the actor is expected to create a physical life."[2] This is a pretty powerful tool to be aware of. The debate of whether this is necessary for the actor is one that will go on till the end of time. I am simply making you aware of the possibilities and capabilities at your command if you so choose.

51. Clip Art

Peruse a number of magazines and newspapers. An old copy of *National Geographic* would be especially useful for this activity. Cut out a number of pictures that evoke powerful feelings within you. For example, you might cut out a picture of the Statue of Liberty that evokes powerful feelings of freedom, honor, and democracy. You might cut out a picture of a beautiful hillside that evokes feelings of serenity, calm, and living a peaceful existence. See if you can find a minimum of five pictures that stir you in some way.

Separate the pictures and put them in various parts of the room. Go up to each image, one at a time, and spend a minimum of one minute with each one. See if you are able to have each image evoke its powerful feelings consecutively. Don't force these feelings; rather, observe what is present within you. You might go up to the Statue of Liberty picture that evokes freedom, liberty, and democracy. Immediately afterwards you may go up to the picture of the hills, which automatically evokes calm, peace, and serenity. This exercise is more

---

[2]Moni Yakim, *Creating a Character* (New York: Watson-Guptill Publications, 1990), 1.

profound if the five pictures each evoke a different set of feelings. In other words, choosing five pictures that all evoke feelings of freedom and liberty is not the aim of this exercise.

Variables:

Find five items around your house that evoke powerful feelings within you and then continue with the exercise.

Discussion:

What was the most important "Eureka!" moment you had during this exercise?

Where did you find your pictures for this activity?

Would this activity be equally successful if you used photos from a family album?

Did the length of time you spent with each photo change the intensity of feelings you felt?

Purpose:

To highlight the power of pictures and images

In this exercise you are asked to choose pictures and images that stir an emotional response within you. What is exciting about this is that the way you respond is often automatic. This is very important information that can be manipulated by a director and an actor. A director might put up a backdrop of a beautiful mountain covered in snow knowing it will stir feelings within an audience. A film director can manipulate the cinematography in precisely the same way. What is also interesting to note is that certain pictures and images will evoke certain feelings within an actor and can therefore be utilized by the director/actor in the same fashion.

To explore the rapid response and change of the body

It is very powerful to find five pictures that can evoke such powerful and contrasting responses in such a short period of time. It is also powerful to be a bystander to the workings of your inner mind and body. You don't have to do anything; your body will respond on its own. One of the aims of the actor in the craft is to develop automatic responses without having to create them. This is a complex process that requires a lifetime of work. This exercise allows you to experience those automatic responses without any preparation. As you continue to grow as an actor, you'll want to build on a vast set of resources from which to work. I must clarify here that being a working actor does not necessarily make you an actor. It is true that if you reach this bracket that you have made some achievements and are in a selected group. The challenge is that if your acting is amateur, novice, or meaningless, your audience may find your acting laughable and pointless. If you are going to be an actor, why not put meaning and depth into your craft?

52. Anatomical Awareness

Find a picture of the muscular system of the human body. You can find this in poster form or in a good anatomy book. You are looking for an anatomical chart of the human body that shows the muscles front and back. On this picture, all the muscles of the human body should be labeled. There are over two hundred muscles in the human body, and I am not asking you to learn them all — I just want you to start to become familiar with some of the muscles.

Now, experiment a little. Pick up a drink and bring it to your mouth. As you bend your arm and bring the drink to your mouth, see if you can figure out what muscles you used to do so. See if you can bring the drink to your mouth without engaging your bicep in some way. Actors have found in the past that it is virtually impossible to do this motion without engaging the bicep. It is also interesting to see which muscles relax while others switch on. For instance, when you bend your arm to bring your drink to your mouth, notice what happens to your triceps. You will find that they have gone into a relaxed state. Experiment with other actions such as picking up a book or walking down the street. While you may not know what all the muscles are, by referring to your chart you should be able to figure out some of the names of the muscles involved and what they are doing.

Variables:

Put on some music and dance freely around your living room. See if you can figure out some of the muscles engaged in this exercise.

Discussion:

Were you surprised how many muscles were involved in some relatively simple tasks?

Did you learn more about where muscles are on your body?

Can understanding the muscles influence the actor's work in any way?

Are you intrigued in any way by the complexities of the human body?

Purpose:

To develop body awareness

You have heard it mentioned time and time again that the actor's instruments are the mind and body. By becoming familiar with the muscles of your body, you are becoming more familiar with your instrument. You might wonder if understanding your muscles and what they do has a direct effect on your acting. If you were on-stage/set thinking about your muscles and what they are doing, this would be detrimental to your acting, but if in your own spare time you experimented with exercises and made your discoveries this way, then you would open up a whole new world of possibilities. When you are performing you forget all of this, but your subconscious does not. Everything the mind and body has learned becomes a part of you.

To increase your capacity to learn

In this exercise you are asked to become familiar with the muscles of the body. You are not asked to learn them all, but you will certainly end up learning some of them. In your acting you are constantly being asked to learn and digest. You may have to learn dialog, positioning, or the context of the scene, to name a few things. Because the projects are constantly changing, you will constantly be learning as an actor. This exercise takes the learning muscle and flexes it. It encourages you to expand your learning capacity. Sometimes you have to look at the bigger picture of acting to see how something that appears to have nothing to do with acting has everything to do with acting.

53. Hot Tub

For this exercise, make yourself a nice, cozy bath. Get in your bath and lie absolutely still. Now see if you can change your perception of the temperature of the water with your thoughts alone. Close your eyes (Be careful not to fall asleep). Can you, through your imagination, allow the water temperature to feel somewhat cooler and send a shiver down your spine? Does the water feel somewhat uncomfortable in its coolness? Can you sense the formation of goose bumps on your arms? Once you have spent a few minutes doing this, open your eyes and move your arms and legs a little. Bring your body back to neutrality.

Now close your eyes again and, as the water reaches stillness, imagine you are in water that is uncomfortably hot. Can you feel the temperature rising throughout your body? Are there sweat beads running down your forehead? Is there a slight sensation of dizziness due to the heat? Are your muscles feeling somewhat tingly and relaxed? Spend a few minutes on this and then shake it out and bring your body back to a neutral state. Enjoy the rest of your bath as you review your findings.

Variables:

Repeat this activity in the sauna or the Jacuzzi and see if you can relay the feelings of coolness to your body. Are you able to take a sauna and actually shiver?

Discussion:

Is it possible that your thoughts can be translated into physical realities?

What is the most important aspect of this exercise?

How is this exercise useful for your acting as a whole?

What is more important, the journey or the end results?

Purpose:

To explore the presentational approach to acting

In this exercise you are being asked to explore your mind to influence your body. As Uta Hagen says, "The presentational actor attempts to reveal human behavior through a use of himself, through an understanding of himself and consequently an understanding of the character he is portraying."[3] In your attempt as an actor to explore human behavior it is necessary for you to continue to explore and discover in every way. The exploration part of this activity is more important than the actual results. Let's say that your aim to create the sensation of feeling cold in the bath fails. You can always come back to the activity and try again. Eventually you will be able to create this sensation, but, more importantly, the lessons you will have learned along the way will be invaluable.

To create body awareness

In order to explore this activity you have to pay attention to what your

[3]Uta Hagen, *Respect for Acting* (New York: Macmillan Publishing Company, 1973), 12.

body is saying and doing. As you start to warm up, you may notice that you are starting to sweat, your pulse rate is increasing, and your head feels slightly faint. As you cool down, the hair on the back of your head may start to stand up, and you may have goose bumps all over. Body awareness is so important for the actor because it allows you to be aware of unnecessary tensions in the body. If you are aware of these tensions, there is more opportunity to address them and allow them to dissipate. For character work you want the capability to make specific physical isolations to suit your character. The clearer your body awareness, the more potential there is for you to achieve this.

54. Arm Extensor

For this exercise find a nice comfortable space where you can lie down on the floor. Make sure your space has a pretty smooth surface so your back is almost flat against the floor. Please make sure your legs are straight out and not at a forty-five degree angle. Close your eyes and take your arms up ninety degrees towards the ceiling. Your biceps should now be by your ears, and your arms should be straight (not locked at the elbows). Keeping your arms straight, slowly start to take them backwards towards the floor behind you — the same direction they would be going if you were doing a backstroke. The key to this exercise is to move very, very slowly. When you think your fingertips are just about to touch the floor, hold that position for thirty seconds. Then continue to move your arms backwards until they actually touch the floor. You may be quite surprised by the results.

Variables:

If you are feeling particularly athletic you can take your legs up to a ninety-degree angle and then lower your legs behind you. Your legs should move slowly past your ears as they lower towards the ground. If you have done this correctly, your body will now be folded in half. Please make sure you are thoroughly warmed up before attempting this exercise.

Discussion:

Were you surprised at how far your arms actually stretched?
Did reaching the floor start to feel as if it were a never-ending mission?
Were you moving your arms slow enough? If you felt you were going too fast, did you repeat the exercise?

Purpose:

To expand your perceptions and understanding

Many actors find when exploring this activity that when they feel they are about to touch the floor there is still a long way to go. They often comment that it feels as if their arms are going way beyond where they perceived the floor to be. Their physical and mental perception of reality differs from actual reality. Let's say you are performing a play that is supposed to be set in a castle. The set designer has done a great job, and yet your castle is still made of cheap wood that is then painted to look like brick. Logic tells the audience that this is not a real castle, and yet through strong acting that sparks their imagination, an audience can be persuaded to suspend logic for a new perception and understanding. You can transport your audience anywhere you want if you can transport yourself there first.

Mind and body connection

In this exercise your mind may believe you are about to touch the floor while your body may be telling you that your arms are sinking way past where the floor should be. What this activity highlights is the mind-body connection. It tells us that we cannot separate the two, for they work in conjunction with each other, if not necessarily in harmony. No matter how sure you are mentally that you are about to touch the floor, the physical reality makes a different case. Make your own link between mind and body and the important role it plays in the craft of acting.

Chapter 10
Physical Attention

55. Seasonal Sensations

For this exercise, act out different sensations such as cold, hot, freezing, warm, sweltering, etc. To act out being hot, for example, you are going to have to ask yourself a number of questions: Just how hot is it? Is it a dry heat or a damp heat? Where exactly are you — in the desert, on a garden bench, or in the sauna? Are the clothes you are wearing cooling you down or adding to your level of discomfort? You may find that the level of heat is causing your clothes to stick to your skin, or perhaps there is sweat trickling from your right armpit. Is your forehead soaking wet? What is the state of your hair and the rest of your clothes? Is your skin burning with the intensity of the sun? Again, be specific. The heat of sitting in the sauna can be soothing and relaxing for many, while the heat of sitting in your car with your AC broken in five miles of backed-up traffic at 105 degrees can be a rather unpleasant experience. It is also possible that you have suddenly become physically hot because of an event or circumstance. If you have ever heard the term, "hot-tempered," you know exactly what I mean. Perhaps an argument with a neighbor or the man who just reversed into your car could cause you to feel hot.

There are plenty of options to choose from; all I ask is that you make specific choices. If you have chosen to recreate the feeling of being hot, then continue to explore this activity until you can actually recreate the feeling of heat in your body and skin temperature. It may take you a number of practices to get there, but eventually, with practice you will succeed. If you do not think it is possible to change the temperature of your body, then ask yourself what happens when someone "sends a chill down your spine." You literally go cold throughout your body, even if only momentarily. When you are embarrassed by something, your face goes red and a hot flush momentarily takes over your body. Instead of recreating the sensation of being hot for the sake of this exercise, you could create a task to give the process an added dimension. For example, you could be in a rush to finish mowing the lawn or fixing a car in your sweltering mechanic shop.

Variables:

Next time you go to the sauna or steam room and you are sitting in sweltering heat, see if you can recreate a chill down your spine or shivers throughout your body.

Discussion:

What enabled you to take this activity from a thought to a physical reaction?

What was the most challenging part of this activity?

If you found that you were able to perspire when recreating the feeling of being hot, did you feel like you had succeeded in the exercise? Justify your answer.

Purpose:

To be able to manipulate your body at a physiological level

This is a very complicated thing to achieve — to not only have an external understanding of action, but to also have an internal understanding of your body's inner working. This exercise allows you to become more intimate with yourself; it gives you a little more knowledge of how your body functions. The more understanding and control we have of our bodies, the better able we are to express through them. As an actor you know that the only instrument you have to play is the one you came into this world with. The more you understand how your instrument works, the more you can create possibilities for growth.

To utilize your imagination to its maximum potential

Through this activity you are going to learn to maximize your imagination. The more contradictory you can make this activity, the more challenging it will become. Let's say you are in your living room and outside it is 105 degrees of Texas heat. Your air conditioner is broken, and you have decided to recreate the sensation of being freezing cold. If, under these circumstances, you are able to send actual shivers down your spine, then you have stretched your imagination to an extreme degree. Let's say you are on a film set with seventy-five crewmembers all around you and you are supposed to be stranded all alone on a desert island. The more you are able to utilize your imagination to its full potential, the easier and more realistic it will become. *The American Heritage Dictionary* defines imagination as, "The formation of a mental image of something that is neither perceived as real nor present to the senses."[1] The challenge for the actor is that you must create a sense of reality from which you allow your imagination to soar. If you do not believe you are on a desert island, why would your audience?

[1] *The American Heritage Dictionary* (New York: Houghton Mifflin Company, 1993), 677.

56. Color Me This

Sit in your bedroom and notice the colors in the room. Observe the color of the walls and take a few minutes to notice what effects the color has on your body and emotions. Now, go into a room that is painted in a different color, sit there for a few minutes, and see what effect that has on you. Now, take a brighter bulb and put it in your bedroom light. What effect does that have on you? Next, turn your bedroom light off completely, sit in total darkness, and see what effect it has on your emotions and body.

If you would like to experiment with a variety of colors, you can buy some cheap tissue paper and stick that up on your wall and notice how it makes you feel. You could also go in a bookstore and simply page through an art book that is full of a variety of colors and stay with each one for a few minutes. I am sure that you have heard of color therapy and that different colors affect people in different ways. Many people find that a pale blue is calming and soothing while a bright red can create anger and stress. Make notes on your findings and review the significance of these results for you.

Variables:

Pick up pieces of fabric that are made out of different material such as cotton, wool, and Velcro. Close your eyes and hold them one at a time and see how each one affects you.

Discussion:

Did any color create feelings of anger in you?
Which color did you find the most calm and tranquil?
What was the most surprising aspect of this activity for you?
How much time did you devote to this activity?
When you do it again, how might you rework it?

Purpose:

To work with external factors to create an organic response

Colors can change the way you are thinking and feeling. If they can have this effect on you in life, can you imagine how exciting it is to manipulate colors during a performance? They can influence not only your acting but also the organic responses of your audience. Bertolt Brecht used very bright, stark lighting for his play, *Mother Courage*, to make his audience feel hot and uncomfortable. His aim was to draw them from the audience into the play, and from all accounts he succeeded. The way that colors and light can change your moods is an important tool for you to be aware of as an actor. I have said that these responses are organic because you will find yourself reacting automatically to a color without the need to plan or create a reaction. There are so many ways that color can be utilized throughout a play or movie, and the actor should have a new found respect for what this can do.

To think outside the box

A number of actors who I have worked this exercise with initially think it sounds a bit silly. It is only by thinking outside of the box and experiencing the results that they can truly judge its value. As an actor, it is imperative that you allow yourself to think outside the box in order to be open to new discoveries. Until you are able to buy into possibilities, you may miss out on opportunities and experiences you never knew existed. Most of your friends are going to think you are crazy to choose a career as an actor because of the number of people in this field who do not successfully realize their dreams. The simple fact that you are willing to take a chance means you are living outside the box. An individual who thinks outside the box is a creative individual, and this is also a necessity for the actor.

57. Fickle Face

This exercise is one I picked up by watching a documentary on a famous Indian actor. He would stand in front of a mirror and practice making as many different facial expressions as he could. He said that there was no expression available to a human being that he could not make. He then proceeded to go through all of the expressions on film. It was quite a treat to watch, and it only took him about one minute.

Stand in front of a mirror and see how many different faces you can make. I want you to name each face by saying, "This is my happy face," "This is my sad face," "This is my angry face," "This is my mischievous face," "This is my depressed face," "This is my unsure face," and so on. You do not have to say this out loud; just define each expression separately. Once you have come up with as many different expressions as you can think of, go through them all again, this time as fast as you can without analyzing or naming each face. Then move away from the mirror and into another room and do the same thing again. Make as many different facial expressions as you can possibly come up with. For a final time, go back to the mirror, do the activity once again, and see if you have come up with any new facial expressions.

Variables:

Contort your body (without injuring it) in as many different ways as you can think of. Notice how you feel mentally and physically as you morph yourself into each different contortion.

Discussion:

How many different facial expressions were you able to come up with?

Did you find there were any facial expressions you were unable to define?

Did you make any new discoveries when you worked without the mirror?

How did varying your pacing change this activity for you?

Purpose:

To define facial expressions as you see them

Every day as you go through life, people will be making many facial expressions and each one of them will mean something. In this exercise you are being asked to define each expression separately to highlight the point that each expression we see from other people registers some sort of meaning for us. If someone walks past you and smiles, it may have a number of meanings such as, "he is friendly," "he seems fake," "she looked tense," or "she seemed to be angry about something." You need to define your facial expressions because facial expressions are defined by other people all the time. I want you to come up with as many as you can because it is a reminder of how expressive and versatile your facial muscles really are. It is so important for an actor to comprehend that every single facial expression she makes on camera or on-stage has some form of meaning to her audience. While this exercise asks you to make facial expressions without any particular justification, this cannot be the case in your acting. Being able to define facial expressions allows the actor to realize that everything he does facially is definable to his audience, whether he likes it or not.

To connect the physical with the emotional

Each time you change facial expressions, you will find that your body also changes in terms of how you feel. Your angry face may create tension and a constricting feeling throughout your body. Your happy face may allow you to feel lightheaded and breathe clearly. Your focused face may allow you to feel centered and grounded. Of course, there is no such thing as a happy face; rather it is a reflection of the motivation or reaction or thought that got you there. However, by mimicking a happy face, you get to experience the reactions in your body at a chemical and physiological level. This can be an eye opener for the actor because it tells us that even through mimicking and using purely external actions we can create internal reactions.

58. Taste Buds 2

This activity is very similar to Exercise 50: Taste Buds (page 104), but it has an important enough variable that I have put it here on its own. Take a plain piece of bread in your hand as before, only this time, instead of transferring to another piece of food, you'll work with hunger and contentment. Begin by closing your eyes and thinking of a time when you were absolutely starving. Let's imagine you haven't eaten since yesterday. Your stomach is growling, aching, and absolutely famished. It feels like so long ago since you last ate you have almost forgotten what food tastes like. As you start to think of this piece of bread, you want to rip it to pieces and devour it; you are absolutely starving and can't wait another second. When you reach this climatic point, devour your piece of bread. Don't leave even a tiny morsel; if you have prepared correctly this shouldn't even be an issue. Once you are finished, open your eyes, move around for a moment, and shake everything out.

Take another piece of bread, sit down in your familiar chair, and close your eyes. This time think of a time when you were absolutely stuffed and could not eat another thing. Your stomach was so bloated you thought it was going to explode. You had eaten so much you could not eat even a sunflower seed. When you get to this point, put your piece of bread in your mouth and eat. It should be uncomfortable and difficult to digest, and yet I want you to recreate the sensation of eating on a very full stomach. When you are finished and find you cannot eat any more, open your eyes and shake everything out. Review your findings for this exercise.

Variables:

See Exercise 50: Tastes Buds (page 104).

Discussion:

Were you able to come up with a personal reference for both parts of this exercise?

Did you feel that closing your eyes enabled you to recreate these sensations in a clearer fashion? Explore your answer.

How can you improve on this exercise?

Purpose:

To change the outcome depending on the circumstances

By changing the circumstances in this exercise, you were for the most part able to change the outcome. All you had was a plain piece of bread, and yet I am hoping you found that it tasted drastically different depending on the circumstances. When you were starving, the piece of bread should have tasted quite special. It is also sometimes the case that when we are overly hungry we lose all appetite. When you were bloated, the piece of bread became your enemy, and there was nothing you wanted less than eating it. Both situations were totally different, and both influenced your feelings about the piece of bread. Let's say you are playing a character who is walking to work. If she only has five minutes to arrive, she may start to run. If, on the other hand, she is fifteen minutes early, she may slow down and look in the shop windows along the way. The outcome is in part dependent on the circumstances.

To use your brain

In order to create the scenario with the bread you have to create the desired situation using your brain. Too often in acting these days the director does not demand much from the actor. They prefer to tell actors exactly what to do instead of allowing them to make their own discoveries. And yet, if an actor is not required to use his own brain, he will merely become a puppet. As Deepak Chopra explains, "If you think of the human brain as the fortress at Machu Picchu, then it, too, must have runners to carry its commands to the farthest outposts of its empire."[2] Even when a director wants to serve you everything on a plate, you can still choose to use your own brain without explaining that you are doing so. An actor is a creative spirit who should be encouraged to blossom and not wither away.

[2]Deepak Chopra, *Quantum Healing* (New York: Bantam Books, 1990), 54.

59. Frozen

For this exercise, find yourself a comfortable space. Set an alarm for seven minutes time and then proceed to stand absolutely frozen for the full seven minutes. Stand absolutely still so that not even your eyelids are moving (this may be quite a challenge). There should be no flinching, scratching, twisting, foot tapping, or any other type of body movement. You may be better off waiting until you have the house to yourself to work on this exercise. If this is not possible, go into your room and close the door so you can concentrate. Once you have completed the assignment, review your findings.

Variables:

Lie on the floor and work this stillness exercise in the same way. It is better that you do this in the daytime so that you do not simply fall asleep.

Discussion:

Were you able to create stillness in your eyelids?
Was there anything calming about creating stillness in your body?
Did absolute stillness change your way of thinking at all?
What was the most challenging aspect of this activity?

Purpose:

To create body awareness

In this exercise you're asked to control your body so that you can create absolute stillness. In acting, you are also asked to control your body so that it can become absolutely free. For instance, if during filming you are twisting your leg because of nerves, this will draw focus and be interpreted to mean something to the audience. The only movement that should be happening within your character is movement that is justified. If there is no purpose for something to be happening, it should not be happening. By standing absolutely still, you get to experience full control over your body. You also become acutely aware of even the slightest movement within your body. This is because you have been asked to put all your focus in this direction. Normally we have a thousand and one other things to focus on, whereas in this exercise you only have this one thing to focus on. The more aware you are of your body now, the less you will need to focus on it later.

To put the body back into balance

While this is not a relaxation exercise, there is something that can be quite relaxing about it. Putting the body into a state of stillness is almost as if you are asking the mind to do the same thing. In meditation you are encouraged to guide your mind into a state of stillness. The lifestyle of an actor or drama student can be quite a stressful one. Even relocating to a city such as London, New York, or Los Angeles can be stressful in itself. You should take any opportunity you have to put balance back into your body. While all those around you may be running around stressed and depressed, why don't you take a step back and enjoy the journey?

Chapter 11
Unlimited Possibilities

60. Twisterama

Are you ready to do some physical exercise? Raise your arms out to your sides so that they are in one straight line. If you look over your right shoulder you should now be able to see directly down the line of your middle finger and the same should be true on your left side. With your arms in this fixed position, twist your upper body towards your right shoulder and see how far you can turn your arms behind you. Make sure you keep your arms straight and your hips squarely facing forward as you attempt this. Make a mental note of how far you were able to turn.

Sit for a minute in a nice comfy chair and close your eyes. Picture yourself doing the activity you just did, only this time, visualize your arms going much further. Perhaps they go so far that the right hand is facing the back wall or even beyond. Picture your arms going way, way past where they just went. Repeat this visualization at least three times.

When you are done, go to the same spot where you were previously, put your arms in the same fixed position, and see how far you can turn them this time. For most of you there should be an improvement in how far you are able to turn your arms. The imagery exercise gives your brain a new set of references from which to work instead of preconceived and limiting ideas of how far you previously thought you would be able to turn.

Once you have completed this activity let the results sink in. It is quite profound to see how your mind can have such powerful influences over your body in such a short period of time.

Variables:

Another way of doing this activity is to simply turn your head over one shoulder, looking back as far as you can. Once you have closed your eyes and done your visualization, repeat the process as before. You do not have to sit down to do the visualization but can stay standing in the same place if you prefer.

Discussion:

Was there a big difference between how far you could turn your arms on the second occasion as opposed to the first?

How important a tool is the mind for the actor?

Purpose:

To stretch the imagination

In this exercise your mind starts off with a preconceived idea of how far it will allow your arms to twist. You may not be consciously thinking this, but a decision has been made on your behalf. When you purposefully put a picture in your mind of having your arms twist further, you are planting a seed. There is no guarantee that your arm twisting will change significantly, but for many of you this may in fact be the case.

Not only has your imagination been stretched, but the results are tangible and right before your eyes. It is so important for each and every actor to realize the power of imagination. To be able to stretch your imagination to its wildest limits will allow you to make breakthroughs you never knew possible. With the continuation and growth of special effects it appears that the skills of the actor are less important and utilized less, yet it is precisely because these special effects are added in after the fact that the actor's imagination needs to be more open and receptive than ever before.

To contradict the limitations of your own mind

When you complete this exercise the first time, your mind already has a preconceived notion of how far your arms are going to twist. For the vast majority of you this notion will change once you have done the visualization. Your mind now has a whole new set of references to work with. When you are in a play or movie, you may find yourself making preconceived judgments about your character. You might find you have made clear-cut choices about how a certain scene needs to be played. It is good to make firm decisions; the challenge comes when these are intractable and you leave no space for growth or discovery. This exercise shows you that your preconceived ideas can be contradicted, and the same goes for your acting. Always be open to making new discoveries and encouraging them to take place right up until the last moment.

61. Alphabet Soup

Find a quiet place to work. Recite the alphabet backwards. Do this out loud while you are up and moving around. It sounds easy enough, but your ultimate aim is to say the entire alphabet in one continuous stream without stopping. You are going to find that at first you have to keep stopping to remind yourself of the next letter. After a few rounds, set a rule for yourself that if you have to stop for any reason, you have to begin again, entirely from scratch. Keep going with this activity until you can complete it. Give yourself a finite deadline for completion, such as a week.

If you find this quite easy (perhaps you learned it as a child), let me up the ante a little bit. Complete the same exercise, only this time perform it in a crowded and busy environment such as a house party, a nightclub, or a busy fast food line. This time, say the alphabet in your head rather than out loud. If you pause for any reason, you must start the entire alphabet again.

Variables:

You could try this exercise with astrological signs, months of the year, or a list of words beginning with each letter of the alphabet. The easier you find this activity, the more challenging you should make it.

Discussion:

How many letters did you get right on your first attempt?

Did you find yourself getting stuck at the same letter?

At what point did the activity become easier for you? Can you pinpoint a reason why?

How long did it take you to complete this activity?

At any point, did you just give up? At what point do you just give up in your acting?

Purpose:

To enhance your learning capabilities

Did you notice that in the first part of this exercise I asked you to say the letters out loud and move around? There is a method to my madness. If you only say the letters in your head, you will be using a very limited range of modalities. By saying the letters out loud you get to both hear and speak the letters. By moving around you get to energize your body and feel the letters in a kinesthetic sense. What we are doing in this activity is utilizing the different tools available to enhance your learning capabilities.

The second part of this activity is made more difficult for you in every way — this time you can only say the letters to yourself, and you are put in a crowded and noisy environment. Many schools of thought will tell you to learn your lines as you rehearse and many will tell you to learn your lines before the first rehearsal ever begins. I am not going to tell you what to do; however, if you are working in television, you may find that rehearsal time is extremely limited. There are a number of actors who learn their lines by sitting down and moving a piece of paper from one line to the next. They also say the lines silently to themselves and memorize them "rope fashion." Some actors find this a very effective approach, but many find it incredibly time consuming and monotonous. Think about it — if you learn your lines in this fashion, virtually none of the tools available to you are being utilized. You don't say the lines, or hear the lines, or feel the lines by moving and energizing the body. It gets even more challenging when you actually have to get up and connect the lines with movement, let alone motivations and justifications. This activity gives you the opportunity to utilize your mind and body to enhance your learning capabilities. The connection between learning and drama is a powerful one. Sue Jennings says, "Another curious misconception about drama is that only the bright children can be truly imaginative; I have often found the reverse, that the response of bright groups tends to be highly conventional and unoriginal while the groups of those of lesser academic ability have fewer preconceived ideas of what they 'should' do."[1] There are those who say acting is purely a gift, yet there is a tremendous amount of learning and growing involved.

To overcome challenges

You are not only asked to attempt this exercise, but to actually complete it. There is a big difference between these two requests. In the first one you might decide to give up at some point, whereas in the second one you know that you have to keep going until you find a way. This is such a wonderful analogy for actors, as so much of what you do depends on your ability to overcome challenges. You may have already faced a great deal of rejection at the audition process, or you may find yourself in this position in the near future. If you simply give up because you can't take the rejection, your acting career is over. If, on the other hand, you learn from your experiences and move on, you will be just fine. Many actors give up their dreams not because of lack of talent but because of lack of imagination. If something isn't working for you, you need to adapt, change, and persevere. In this exercise you can use this same philosophy.

---

[1]Sue Jennings, *Remedial Drama* (London: Pitman Publishing, 1973), 36.

62. Driving Delights

Find a day when you are driving and you are stuck in gridlock traffic. If you do not drive, you can perform this exercise as passenger. This day should also be a day when you are full of frustration and anger — when being stuck in traffic is absolutely infuriating and the last thing that you need. When you are having one of these days, only then may you begin this exercise.

Find a way to have an absolutely delightful journey. Come out of your traffic-filled drive absolutely ecstatic, relaxed, and fulfilled. This is going to be quite a challenge; nevertheless, this is your mission, should you choose to accept it.

How are you going to complete this exercise? Utilize any experience in your imagination that will allow you to accomplish this. Perhaps you can imagine a time when you were at the beach, totally relaxed, and sitting by the ocean. How about that time you were leaving work or school and getting ready for a two-week vacation and nothing else mattered or could ruin your day? Maybe you could sit in traffic and enjoy the fact that you can use this time to quietly contemplate your journey as an actor and how exciting the future can be.

Here's a hint as to how you will know if you are succeeding in this activity: If you find you are taking shallow breaths and the muscles in your neck are tense, then you are not succeeding. If, on the other hand, you are breathing calmly and deeply, developing a soft smile, and your eyes feel soft and relaxed, you are probably on your way. In other words, you should be experiencing the results at a physiological level. You will be able to feel when you are succeeding in your aims and when you are not. If you are not able to achieve this for the entire journey, rework this activity on another occasion. I only want you to utilize this activity when you are feeling absolutely frustrated and impatient with the traffic before you. As a note of caution, it stands to reason that I want you to stay focused on the road at all times — safety first!

Variables:

Come up with your own.

Discussion:

What was the turning point when the traffic no longer affected you?

How did the thoughts and situation you chose serve to calm you and allow you to enjoy the journey? What other places in your life would thoughts such as these be useful to you?

Did you find that your journey went more quickly when you experienced it in a positive sense?

Purpose:

To go against the grain

In a situation such as gridlock traffic, it is quite normal for you to get frustrated and irritated. In this exercise you are being asked to look past that fact and find a way to enjoy the journey. This is something that is probably almost foreign to you in circumstances such as these. When you are playing a scene, stop and think before jumping for the obvious. Let's say you are playing the part of a high school dropout, so you decide that this means the character is uneducated and fairly simple. If you think about the fact that Henry Ford had a limited education and Bill Gates dropped out of college, you would realize that some of the most brilliant minds are "uneducated." Dig beneath the surface of your character or the scene and see what you can discover.

To break through new barriers

It is quite exciting to find yourself enjoying a journey that a moment before you were absolutely loathing. When you find that by using your imagination you are able to do just this, the results are quite empowering. Breaking through this barrier allows you to use this experience to help you break through other limitations in your acting. By breaking down previously conceived ideas about the limitations in your acting, you are able to stretch the boundaries further and further. Rehearsals are a good place for actors to make new discoveries which, once made, cannot be undone. The only limitations on actors are the ones they place on themselves.

63. Thumbs Up

Sit down in a comfortable chair, place your hands behind your head, and link your fingers together. Without unlacing your fingers, bring your hands over your head and place them on your knees. Whichever thumb has landed on top is your dominant thumb. This is the exercise in its entirety. When you are finished, think about the significance of this activity.

Variables:

Sit in a chair and cross one leg over the other. Don't think; cross over whichever leg feels the most natural. The results of this exercise could, in fact, be related to you having one hip slightly more rotated than the other, so the way you cross your legs may be subconsciously related to comfort.

Discussion:

Can you think of any value at all in this exercise?

If an exercise is very short in its exploration, can the findings still be significant?

Did you find that your dominant thumb is the same as your dominant hand?

Were you surprised at which thumb came out on top? Explain your answer.

Purpose:

To explore the link between the subconscious and acting

The reason I had you link your hands behind your head is because the thumb that went on top did so subconsciously. It is your dominant thumb because it is stored as such in your long-term memory. Do a little experiment for me. Put your hands behind your head and this time purposefully and methodically put your other (non-dominant) thumb on top. It is going to feel a little awkward. This is because it is not programmed to be that way in your subconscious.

How does the subconscious link to acting? I believe that there is an enormous amount of work and exploration to do in regards to the subconscious and acting that will take years of exploration. For now, let's think about a few areas of interest. Everything that has ever happened to you is recorded and stored in your brain. Have you ever found yourself watching a movie that you have not seen in ten years and suddenly know the next line or the next scene? This is because we have recorded all of our experiences and we are the sum of all our experiences. Milton Erickson, who is arguably the most influential hypnotherapist of all time, observes, "And it is very important for a person to know their subconscious is smarter than they are. There is a greater wealth of stored material in the unconscious."[2] The more we can

[2]Milton Erickson, Ernest L. Rossi, and Sheila I. Rossi, *Hypnotic Realities* (New York: Halstead Press, 1976), 9.

understand about our subconscious, the more we can understand why we do the things we do. Have you ever heard a friend say, "I don't know why I always go out with the same type of guys," or, "Why does this always happen to me?" There is a subconscious link to all of our patterns of behavior; however, the answers can be stored deep within us. The reason I raise this topic in relation to acting is that it allows us to touch on the concept of why people do the things they do. The subconscious can affect motivation.

To open our acting to new possibilities

In this very basic exercise we discover that our long-term memory has information stored whether we know it or not. This opens up our imagination when we start to think about all the other processes in which our mind makes these automatic decisions for us. It is not necessarily always as literal as this exercise; nonetheless, it is happening all the time. A big part of the reason that some individuals smoke is because they have formed a habit of smoking, even when they tell themselves they would like to quit. This is a habit that has been formed and accepted by their long-term memory. When they are able to change their attitude towards the habit of smoking, they are able to get rid of this life-threatening habit for good. As we start to have a basic understanding of our subconscious, we are given a new avenue to explore why we do the things we do. As an actor, this will give you a new set of avenues to explore when thinking about why your character does what he does. It will also open you up to the understanding that while our conscious decision-making is vital, it is certainly not the only influential decision-making tool we have. If you are going for an audition you may already have some preconceived ideas that you are not going to get the job; this belief may be stored in your subconscious. If you can recognize this, you can change it. People who have faith allow their faith to permeate deep into their soul to guide them through life. As you guide your way through life, be open to the different factors that make up who you are as a human being.

64. Dance Off

Pick out two songs that you absolutely love. For the sake of this exercise, these songs should both be upbeat in tempo. Play one of the songs and dance, letting go of any inhibitions you might have. Dance as freely as you possibly can for the entire song. Because there is nobody watching you, this should be quite easy to accomplish. Ideally, once you have finished with the first song, you will have danced so hard that you have worked up a little sweat.

Switch to the second song and this time close your eyes as you dance. As you dance, visualize yourself acting out a part, rehearsing, or getting the audition that you wanted. Whatever you choose, it should be in a positive and supporting light. Because you have your eyes closed, move in a smaller area so as to avoid colliding with items around you, but still dance full out and really let yourself go. When you are finished, observe how you are feeling.

Variable:

Instead of visualizing something related to acting, you can visualize anything that you believe will benefit you. Perhaps you could visualize yourself having a wonderful and relaxing day. Allow your imagination to go where it chooses.

Discussion:

Could this activity be described as a freeing exercise?

Explain your findings.

Can dancing increase your potential for developing imaginative thinking?

Was there any point during your dancing that you felt momentarily out of control?

Purpose:

To create the potential for inspiration

When you are dancing, your body is moving in all different directions. If you are able to absolutely let go, it becomes very freeing for you. At some point you may move in such an inspirational manner that you had no idea that you had the potential to do so. There is a point in falling of no return where you must fall. You cannot stop in mid air, and thus it is a moment of freedom. This is potentially true for dancing as well. This is important for the actor because it is in those moments of inspiration that an audience can be mesmerized. This exercise creates a potential frame of reference for inspiration.

To explore the power of visualization

The subconscious mind thinks in pictures and images. This is powerful information because it lets you know that you are able to manipulate what goes into your mind. If you have the ability to influence your mind in any way that helps your acting journey and other areas of your life, then you have the right to do so. Some actors say they don't want to play with their minds; however, it is pretty much impossible to be an actor and not play with your mind. The difference here is you are playing with it rather than it playing with you. The dancing will give you an extra burst of energy and endorphin release that may compound the results of this exercise even further. A person who goes to the gym will generally go back again and again. They realize that exercise is something that needs to be utilized on a regular basis. Work with this exercise as you see fit and see if you achieve your desired results or improve in the situation. Visualization is a powerful part of the actor's work. Eric Morris talks about this sense and says, "Unless we train our vision to be specific, it will limit our perceptions to the overall object."[3] It is important not to limit yourself in any way as an actor; rather, continue to grow.

65. Concentration Zone

For this exercise I hope you are feeling pretty strong. Find a heavy object that you can pick up with one hand. Pick up your heavy object and hold it straight out in front of you at a ninety-degree angle. If the object is very easy to hold out, then it is not heavy enough. If you can only hold it for a couple of seconds, it is too heavy. Be careful to protect your wrist no matter what item you choose. At the same time that you are holding your object, work on some difficult math problems. Some examples are twenty-three times nine, forty-five times eight, and seventy-eight times twelve. If these are math problems that you would never be able to solve, come up with some a little easier. If they are too easy, come up with some that are more complex. The main requirement is that you work out the answer to these problems while holding your heavy object out in front of you. You may find that you are not able to solve the problems. That is absolutely fine; the aim is that you attempt to do so. Once you are exhausted from holding up your heavy object, put it down and see how much easier it is to work out the math problems. Once you are finished review your findings.

[3]Eric Morris, *Being and Doing* (Los Angeles, CA: Spelling Publications, 1981), 93.

Variables:

Instead of working on math problems, spell difficult words or recite a complex monolog. Anything that requires a great deal of concentration can be utilized here.

Discussion:

Was the object you chose to lift up heavy enough?

Did you find that your level of focus became blurred while holding up your heavy object?

Did you feel mentally tired at the end of this activity?

Purpose:

To highlight the destructive role of tension

If you were doing this exercise correctly, you will most likely have found that your concentration became clouded. By creating physical tension in the body, the task of completing the math problems becomes that much more challenging. This is a great frame of reference for you to have. It highlights the idea that an actor who has a great deal of tension in his body cannot function properly in the role. It may lead to you forgetting your lines, failing to hear what is being said, or using false and forced movements. These are just a few of the numerous challenges tension can create. I have, on a number of occasions, heard novice actors ask when they are going to do some real acting. If they do not want to explore the idea of releasing tensions from their body and mind, then I would have to answer, "Never!" Don't confuse this with a little nervous energy that can actually be converted into energy for a performance. I am talking about tensions that can be crippling for the actor — tensions that we often do not even know are there. An actor who is gripping a cup so tight that her veins are popping may have no idea that this extra tension is even there. By being aware of tensions you can learn to release them and enhance your acting.

To guide you into becoming a better actor

At times, when actors work with this exercise they do not immediately see the connection to acting. This is okay because the acting connection is not always on the surface. Sometimes you have to dig a little deeper to get the answers you seek. Sometimes you have to be willing to change your perception of what it means to become a better actor, to become a stronger actor, to become an effortless actor. As the character Haw pondered in *Who Moved My Cheese?*, "He had to admit that the biggest inhibitor to change lies within yourself, and that nothing gets better until you change."[4] If you are finding that your acting is becoming stagnant or lifeless, perhaps it is time to start working in a new or different direction. This exercise is quite basic, and yet at the same time it is quite complex. Its message is an important one, and there are many important lessons for an actor to learn along the way.

66. Glass Half Empty/Glass Half Full

For this exercise you need a pencil and paper. Divide your paper into two sides. Title one side "Glass half empty" and the other side "Glass half full." Make a list of all areas of your life that you would put in the "Glass Half Empty" category. For instance you might say, "I have no money," "I have little confidence," "I lack any formal training in acting; all my friends have more than me." Put down anything that is holding you back. Now turn your attention to the other side of the paper and write down everything about your life that is "Half Full." For example: "I have a kind and supportive family," "I am passionate about acting," "I have good friends," "I am young and have plenty of time," "I live in a free society where anything is possible if I work hard," "I am intelligent and I learn fast." Some actors say that when they start this activity they do not have much to put in the, "Glass Half Full" column. Do you see how this could make life pretty depressing? Keep working until you can put at least five things in the "Glass Half Full" column, even if it takes you an hour to do so.

Now, look at the "Glass Half Empty" column and work out how you can move these things into the "Glass Half Full" column. You may have written down, "I have no training in acting"; think about how you might solve this. Write down some possible solutions: "I will join the theatre group at my school." "I will take an evening workshop." "I will apply for drama school and see if I can receive a scholarship." Let's say you also put on your list, "I have no money." Look for ways to change this: "I will get a job with flexible hours." "I will train in another skill I enjoy that pays fairly well to help support my acting career." "I will spend less money on frivolous things." It is important to note that you do not have to solve all of these challenges today. You are simply going to start working towards them. As long as you are moving forward, you can take as much time

[4]Spencer Johnson M.D., *Who Moved My Cheese?* (New York: G. P. Putnam's Sons, 1998), 72.

as you need. Some people like time limits because it gives them a goal to reach. If this works for you, set realistic timelines that encourage and motivate you. It is also worth noting that some of the things you wrote on your "Glass Half Empty" list may not necessarily belong there. Let's say you put, "I have no money"; perhaps you do not have much money, but are you homeless? Did you eat today? There is a difference between having little money and having no money. Creating more income is certainly something to address; I just want you to be able to put it a little more into perspective. Once you have worked through your list, start to put it into action in your life.

Variables:
Help fellow actors or friends with their lists.

Discussion:
In what way is this exercise empowering for your life?
In what way is this exercise empowering for your acting career?
Why is it important that an actor see his glass as "half full"?
Why is it necessary for actors to be grounded in their lives?
What was the most important breakthrough you got from this activity?

Purpose:
To take action where action is needed
In this exercise you get to make two lists that allow you to see the way you have been viewing things in your life. If you find you have been viewing things fairly negatively, this can weigh quite heavily on your day-to-day life. By taking action, you will be able to take the items on your "half empty" side and move them to the "half full" side. Imagine spending your entire life with an enormous list of "half empties." This will not only be incredibly depressing but also stifle your creativity. Not only will your enjoyment of life suffer, but so will your enjoyment and potential to grow as an actor. As Maxwell Maltz explains, "The person who perceives himself to be a failure type person will find some way to fail in spite of all his good intentions or his willpower, even if opportunity is literally dumped in his lap."[5] A little bit of suffering builds character, but when it becomes the main focus of one's life, it is detrimental to growth. Take action to move your life forward in the ways that serve you best.

[5]Maxwell Maltz, *The New Psycho Cybernetics* (New York: Prentice Hall, 2001), 4.

To change your perspective

It is amazing to note that when we change our perspective we can literally change our lives. I sometimes work with actors who tell me, "I never work; there is no work out there." If you say that statement with enough conviction, often enough you will create your own reality. I have also worked with actors who call themselves "superstars." While they may not yet be superstars, some of these actors never stop working because they have such a belief in their own abilities and who they are. They look at their lives and say, "The glass is half full!" Not only do they say these things, but they work very hard to take action to create the realities they desire. You do not have to be a superstar to have a successful life as an actor, but you do have to enjoy the journey. Acting requires a tremendous amount of energy. Stress, anger, hate, self loathing, and depression also require a tremendous amount of energy. You cannot continuously devote energy to acting and these negative feelings and reach your full potential as an actor. It is your life, and only you can create your own destiny.

Chapter 12

Act and React

67. Telephone Tattle

For this exercise, have a conversation on the phone with yourself. That's right, you read correctly — with yourself. Improvise some dialog on the phone. You can choose any scenario you like; perhaps you are getting directions to the dentist, arranging to pick up your dog from the vet, or speaking to your mother about a dinner party on Friday. Now, I want you to hear the other person's response. I don't mean you should vaguely pretend to hear something in general. If you asked, "What time is my appointment?" by utilizing your imagination you should have heard, "Mrs. Edwards, your appointment is at two o'clock on Wednesday." Hear very specific responses and allow time for those responses and your reactions. I want to make it clear that you are not being asked to phone anyone, and it is better to turn your phone off before starting this activity. While you should be saying your lines out loud, the responses from the other person should simply be heard in your imagination, not vocalized. When you are ready to take a break, go ahead and phone a friend and pay attention to what you do when it is her turn to speak. Listen to the responses and pay attention to what you are doing at that moment. When you have finished your conversation, go ahead and work the exercise again with a completely different scenario.

Variables:

Vary the amount of time you spend on this activity. You might decide that you are going to have a ten-minute improvised conversation. This can be quite a challenge if you are to hear every one of the other person's responses. It will take a great deal of focus and concentration to do this with believability.

Discussion:

What tools did you use to help yourself hear the other person's responses?

At any point did you find yourself zoning out and not hearing your partner's responses?

Did you keep the phone close to your ear or did you simply mimic and pretend to hold it close?

Explore this statement: The ability to listen can be quite draining.

Purpose:

To delve beneath the surface of the script

As an actor you are constantly going to find yourself with scripts that ask you to do some of the work. Many phone conversations will not be written with the luxury of the other person's dialog. Many actors will simply accept this fact and have a one-way phone conversation. This activity encourages you to acknowledge that this is a two-person scene and that you must create dialog for the other person. How can you react to another when you do not know what you are reacting to? When you have a script in front of you, it might also be very beneficial to write in the other person's responses. This activity gets you accustomed to the idea that a script is never really a finished product, but rather it is a beginning. In talking about scriptwriting, Lajos Egri comments, "If the reading public understands the mechanism of writing, if the public becomes aware of the hardships, the tremendous effort that goes into any and all literary work, appreciation will become more spontaneous."[1] It is the actor who must lift the words off of the page and bring them to life. The more proactive you are willing to become in your work, the more far-reaching your results will become.

To act and react

In this activity, you are being asked to listen to your imaginary partner and hear her responses. If you do not hear any responses, you have nothing to respond to. You have a doubly hard job to do, because in this exercise you also have to create lines that are not given to you. Listening is such an important part of acting, and yet you will often see actors neglect this. They will be in a scene, oblivious to the fact that they are supposed to become engaged in dialog with another person, and it appears as if two totally separate conversations are taking place. When you are really listening to another, the inner processes of your reactions cannot help but show themselves in your facial expressions and body language. When you are not listening, there is a forced predictability to your actions and, in many cases, a vacant expression. I have always believed that it is far more difficult to be a bad actor than a fine actor because the bad actor has so little to work with, and his work is always laughable and grotesque in its execution. Listening is an important part of your work as an actor that will allow you to create and make new discoveries on an ongoing basis.

[1]Lajos Egri, *The Art of Dramatic Writing* (New York: Simon and Schuster, 1946), xiii.

68. Listen Logic

Go into the living room, lie on the floor, and close your eyes. Start listening to the inner sounds of your body such as your heartbeat and your breathing. Make sure that you keep your focus only on the areas I ask for. In this case, you should be listening to the sounds of your body and nothing else. If you suddenly begin to notice the sound of a ticking clock, ignore it and allow it to fade away. As you proceed with this exercise, remain on the floor with your eyes closed. After one or two minutes, spread your center of awareness to the room around you. Perhaps you can now hear the ticking of the clock, the creak of the floor, or the sound of the air conditioner. Again, widen your center of awareness to include other rooms in the house. Perhaps you can hear the humming sound coming from the freezer in the kitchen. Begin to spread your awareness even further to include the sounds coming from outside your house. This could include the sound of a passing car or people talking. Finally, I would like you to stretch your awareness as far as it can go — stretch it to its limits. Perhaps you can hear the sound of sirens off in the distance, or a bird chirping faintly. Once you are finished, review your findings and see if you can comprehend the meaning of what you have just done.

Variables:

Let's add one more element and have you listen to the sounds of the world around you and the energy field that is life. You may not hear literal sounds; utilize your imagination.

Discussion:

What was the first sound you heard? Did you find that this sound was more defined and prominent than on a day-to-day basis?

What happened to your focus and concentration as your center of awareness expanded?

Did you discover any sounds that you have not been aware of on a regular basis?

Purpose:

To encourage you to create specific centers of focus

In this exercise you are asked to focus your listening in a very clear and specific way. You may be filming a scene at a train station where you are discussing some very secretive information with a co-conspirator. In this situation, your focus of awareness may need to be directly on this other person. Even though there are sounds of trains and people rushing all around you, these sounds have no place in your line of focus. The importance of your conversation and what is being said keeps your focus firmly planted on your immediate surroundings. It is all too common to see an actor look distracted or lacking in clear focus, and this causes the work to look confused. This can even be applied when you are auditioning. Instead of listening to the director, your focus may be shifted to the scene you are about to perform. You may have missed some valuable notes and, consequently, failed to get the part.

Putting the body back into balance

In this exercise you are asked to focus your attention on the sounds around you. As you focus your attention on these sounds you will find that your body begins to let go. When we put our focus and energy in a given direction there is often no time available to create tension in the body. This is of great value to actors because we always want our bodies to be free of unnecessary tensions. Let's say you are in a movie where you are involved in a fight scene. If you play this scene with all the tension that a fight requires, you will be exhausted after about a minute. If you have to do this scene twenty times in a row, there is no way your body will be able to continue to work so hard for so long. As an actor, your body may have to appear tense for this scene when in fact underneath it all your body is loose and free.

69. Ceiling Stare

For this exercise, go to a busy public place. I prefer that you choose a space that is somewhat limited in size and where people are to some degree confined. When you arrive at your location, stare at the ceiling for at least three minutes. Although I would like you to choose a focal point, you are really staring at nothing in particular. You need to keep your focus on this area while being subtly aware of what the people around you are doing. Are they stopping and looking with you? Did anyone do a double-take as they walked by? If you stay in a somewhat confined area, you will have more opportunity to observe the results. You will almost certainly find that someone will ask you what you are staring at. This is another opportunity for you to utilize your acting skills and your imagination. You can tell them you have seen a spider or you like the ceiling or anything else you can come up with. This has to be convincing, so it will require good acting. Perhaps you can even create a situation that leaves other people staring at the ceiling, even after you've left. If this is the case, observe what is happening from a comfortable distance. Please choose a safe environment in which to work this exercise.

Variables:

Another way of doing this exercise is to take a piece of paper and write in bright colors, "Do not step here." Use a little bit of masking tape, stick the paper on the sidewalk, and see how many people walk around it and how many actually step on it. You might want to laminate it to make it stronger. Observe your findings for this activity. Don't forget to remove your paper and masking tape from the sidewalk when you're finished.

Discussion:

How could you sense when other people were staring at the ceiling as well?

In what way does this activity allow you to manipulate human nature?

How did you manage to stay focused throughout this activity?

Could you have chosen a more beneficial environment to work this activity? Explore your answer.

Purpose:

To understand human behavior

In this exercise you will most likely find that your behavior will influence the behavior of others. In a role, perhaps you are playing a young man who you see as very gentle and kind. In the middle of the script it says he goes to a football (soccer) match with a group of his friends, and after the match he and his friends chase and beat up a fan from the opposing team. This seems very contradictory to you, and you can't quite understand why your character would act this way. It is only when we realize that many people are easily influenced by the behavior of the group that this type of behavior can make perfect sense. An action that would be unspeakable for us to do alone suddenly becomes acceptable when conforming to the masses.

Action and reaction

As you are staring up at the ceiling it is likely that those around you will react by staring up in the same direction. The action of your behavior

141

has caused a reaction in their behavior. In acting there is a wonderful phrase: "Act and react." In other words, your words, actions, and energy should cause the other actors around you to react in kind. Sometimes an actor is simply waiting for the cue line so that she can respond with her own line. This is going to nullify the opportunity to react. If all of her focus is on her lines, it is impossible for her to hear and react to what is being said by the other actors. Some of the most interesting parts of acting are not what a character says but how she reacts to what is being said by others.

Chapter 13
Understanding Your Objective

70. Center of Attention

Pick a person in a café, restaurant, shopping mall, park, or other public place. Choose a person who is not looking at you in any way. Perhaps you are behind him or to the side of him, or he is looking in a totally different direction. See if you can force your focus on him to such a degree that he feels obliged to look in your direction. In order to achieve this, you are going to have to focus all of your concentration and energy in his direction. Your thoughts should be speaking so loudly to him that his ears are burning. Whatever thoughts you choose to use, please keep them pleasant and not intrusive. In other words, I humbly ask you not to think, "Turn around right now or I am going to scream at you." A better thought process might be, "Please turn, please turn right this instant." There is no definitive time limit for this exercise. You may get him to turn in thirty seconds, or it may take you five minutes. If you have tried for a while with one person and nothing happens, feel free to move on to someone else. It is going to take a tremendous amount of focused and specific concentration to start to see results in this activity. Once you have his attention, drop it in an instant and move on.

Variables:

For this variable you are going to need another person. Take a pack of playing cards and have him choose a card without showing you. Now ask him to focus his attention on the card and repeat its description to himself rhythmically and silently. If he is looking at a king of diamonds, he could repeat the phrase "king of diamonds" over and over. You will also need to focus all of your energy in his direction. When you think you know the card, give your answer. This activity can take as long or as little time as you like. You can also try it working with different people to see if you get better results with one person than another.

Discussion:

What was the shortest amount of time it took you to get someone to look at you?

What were the variables you think allowed you to achieve your goal so successfully on that occasion?

What if I suggest to you that the time you spent attempting to get people to look at you is as important as actually achieving the outcome?

Come up with your own answers as to why I might make this suggestion.

What is the significance of this activity for the actor?

Purpose:

To infect your partner

I do not mean that you should pass on a communicable disease. When performing in a scene with another, you should infect them in such a manner that they are forced to respond to you in kind. You can have two actors in a scene working as two separate actors, or you can have two actors who are bouncing off each other. This activity helps you to develop the intensity of communicating with another. The odds of getting your message across and actually having each person turn to face you are against you, and yet you must try with all your heart and soul to do so. This activity will help remind you that in every scene you play you must commit one hundred percent to getting across your character's message and viewpoint. Do not back off, do not quit; everything your character has to say is of great importance. If a line has no value, why bother saying it? If you don't care about what you are saying, why should your audience care?

To know your objective

In this activity you have a very clear objective: get the other person to turn around and look at you. If you don't put all of your energy into making this happen, it is unlikely you will see any results whatsoever. In every scene you are in, even if you have no lines, you must always know your objective. Let's say you have a non-speaking role in a movie, and the director has told you to be in the background and not draw attention to yourself. Now this would be very bad direction, but let's say this is all you've been given. You need to create around this. You must know why you are in the scene, and what your character's driven purpose is.

Let's say that you have a part in a movie that is set in medieval England. In this scene, a public hanging is taking place (very common in those days), and you are one of the spectators. You need to make some very specific choices as to how your character feels about what they are witnessing. Perhaps they love nothing more than a good hanging, or perhaps it repulses them to the depth of their gut. Whatever you do, make definitive choices. If you stand there with absolutely no objective whatsoever, your audience will pick up on it immediately. Dave Allen comments in his book, *Stanislavski for Beginners*, "An objective should be believable and should make you want to carry it out."[1] Your audience is more intelligent than you might give them credit for. They may not always be able to articulate what they are seeing, but almost everyone can pick up on bad acting.

71. Through the Looking Glass

Enter a space in your house/apartment. Each time you enter this space, do so as if it were an entirely different place. On the first occasion you might choose to enter as though it were a cathedral that has a wonderfully high ceiling and stained glass windows. As you come into the cathedral, use your eyes, head, neck, and pacing to explore where you are. Do not mime or act out a charade. For example, don't get down on one knee and cross yourself. Restrict your scene to the way you are looking around the space: this is the most important factor. Some other spaces you might want to enter could be a castle, a prison cell, or a run-down apartment — whatever your imagination can conjure up. There is no audience for this activity. There is no one to tell you whether or not they believe your interpretation, so make sure you utilize all the tools available to you. You could certainly utilize your senses for this exercise. If you are walking into a room in a castle, what does it smell like, what does it look like, how does it feel, what are the sounds you can hear, how do the cobbled stones feel against your feet? How about if you are walking into a four-by-four prison cell — how will your entrance into this space differ? You do not have to indicate any of your findings here, but it is important that your senses are active to bring your imagination to life.

Variables:

On another occasion you might want to work this exercise by having another actor watch you and see if they can tell what space you are entering. At an appropriate point, you can switch places.

Discussion:

When you entered the space, at what point did you really see yourself as being there?

---

[1]David Allen, *Stanislavski for Beginners* (New York: Writers and Readers Publishing, Inc, 1999), 128.

How did the height of the ceiling (real or imagined) affect the way you entered the space?

Were there any people in any of the spaces you entered? Did this enhance or detract from the task at hand?

Purpose:

To know the space you are entering

In this exercise you have to know the space you are entering before you actually come in so that you are mentally prepared. A novice actor will enter a space as if he is walking on to the stage/set and then after a few moments remember it is supposed to be the living room or the dentist's office. The challenge is that by this time it is too late and the momentary lapse in concentration has broken the spell. The audience, in disbelief, is brought back to the reality that this is a stage/set and not a castle/cathedral in any shape or form. It takes a great deal of energy, concentration, and imagination to allow your audience to buy into the space you are creating.

Audition practice

Any time you are about to enter the room for an audition, it is important to remind yourself that your audition starts the moment you set foot in the room. If you enter shyly, walk over slowly, or give a meek wave, your audition is over before it has even begun. Even if you give an outstanding performance you have created doubt in the minds of the director/casting agent, and that will most likely be enough to keep you out of the running. You have heard the phrase "own the audition." This also applies to the space itself: "own it." Unfortunately, you won't get a second chance and, as everyone knows, first impressions count. This exercise brings your attention to the space you are entering, and it is up to you to keep it there.

72. Purpose Driven

For this exercise, mess up your bed. In a minute I am going to ask you to make your bed with three different scenarios in mind. The first time you make your bed, do so with the knowledge that your boyfriend/girlfriend has just broken up with you over the phone. He/she tells you that he/she has met someone else and wanted to be honest with you. How will this knowledge affect the way you fold the sheets? Will it slow you down as you are in an absolute daze at what has just happened? Will your bed be neat and precise, or will it still look like a mess when you are finished? Take about a three-minute break to get your body back to neutrality before starting the second part.

For the second part, make your bed with the knowledge that you are going to work on an expedition in the Amazon and this is that last time you will be sleeping on a bed for a year. As you make your bed, do so with the understanding that it is going to be a long time before you experience this level of comfort again. Do you fold your sheets extra tenderly or lovingly? Is there a newfound level of respect and appreciation for your bed covers? Again, take a short break before continuing with the third part of this exercise.

I think you are going to enjoy this third part. Make your bed as if you've just found out you have been cast in a lead role in a movie. You knew you were up for the role, although getting the part has come as a great surprise to you. Make your bed with this knowledge and see what happens. By the end of this activity you should be very good at making your bed. Review the differences in the way you made the bed each time and ponder your discoveries.

Variables:

Come up with three new scenarios before you make your bed. Or, instead of making the bed, change up the activity. Some possibilities are sweeping the floor, washing the dishes, writing a letter, and eating your breakfast.

Discussion:

How did the given circumstances change the way in which you made the bed each time?

Did you react in ways that were unpredictable for you during this activity?

When making the bed, do you think the essence of what was driving you was coming across?

What were the unexpected results from this activity?

Purpose:

To create purpose-driven responses

In this exercise you are making the bed, but the given circumstances affect the way in which you make the bed. Sometimes you will hear an actor say, "I am going to play this scene angry," but this is a drastic mistake. Anger does not stand alone, but must be driven from a set of circumstances and actions. When you find out your boyfriend/girlfriend has broken up with you, this might lead to great sorrow. You may find you cannot fold the sheets properly and that it takes you three attempts when, under normal circumstances, it would normally take only one. You do not need to "play sorrow"; the fact that your partner has just broken up with you will drive the scene and create the response of sorrow, hurt, anger, betrayal, or whatever comes up for you. Playing an emotion is incorrect; play the scene and the emotional responses will follow.

To create challenges to solve

If you have worked in television, you would find that a lot of challenges are removed from the actor. The fewer props they put in your hands, the easier it is in terms of keeping continuity in the scene. This actually makes the acting more complex for the actor to do realistically because oftentimes we do have things in our hands. It can feel false and forced to be constantly standing around empty handed.

In this exercise you are given a task to do to create challenges for you, to put obstacles in your way. Imagine a wife whose husband says he is going to stay late at the office tonight. As she hears this news she is fuming because he promised he would be home on time tonight. She has the cell phone to her ear, the baby in one hand, and four shopping bags in the other. As she is talking, she drops one of the bags on her foot, the baby starts to scream, and her anger and frustration becomes intensified. If these problems had been given to an actor, they would actually add to the scene and give him a great deal more to work with. Real life is full of real challenges, and when one disappears another one crops up.

73. Direct a Song

Choose a song that you absolutely love. It can be any song as long as it has words. Before you begin this activity, memorize the song so that you can sing it without accompaniment. If you don't feel comfortable with this, you may sing with the background music, but not vocals.

For this exercise, you are going to direct your own song. Look at the lyrics and tell the story. What is the subtext behind the words? What is this song really about? I want you to see your song as a complete picture, a complete story that has a beginning, middle, and end. Don't sing the song for the sake of singing it.

In addition to singing, add some justified movements or choreography to go with this piece. It is not enough to have a beautiful voice; this is a performance. If a line from your song is, "You and I are like the shimmering stars in the sky," what movements would accompany this? It is okay to sit down and plan some of the things you want to do with your song. It is also very beneficial to get up and do it. You will make new discoveries each time you perform the song. It is also beneficial to break your song up into smaller sections and work each section individually. Perhaps you can break your song up into beginning, middle, and end.

When you're satisfied with your performance, take the same song and interpret it in a totally different way. See if you can give your song a whole new meaning. When you are finished, review your findings. Feel free to perform your song for friends at a later date and get their feedback.

Variables:

Sing your song in the bathroom and play with the acoustics. Singing in the bath usually allows those of us who are musically challenged to sound pretty good. This is also a good way to build confidence in your singing. You do not have to become a professional singer, but perhaps this exercise will allow you to become better rounded.

Discussion:

Why did you choose that particular song?

What surprised you most about the subtext you discovered in your song?

What is the significance of being able to work a piece from beginning to end?

What is the importance of the visual aspects in this activity in terms of audience perception?

Purpose:

To work for completion

Let's say you are working on a play or film and you have two lines. There is something very disjointed about this. You are thrown into the middle and make an abrupt departure. Unless you receive lead roles or are in a one-man/woman show, you will be working in this fashion quite consistently. The beauty of directing your own song is that you get to experience the completeness of the piece from beginning to end. A song is not disjointed — it tells a complete story. While you may only have one line in a movie, you need to create some form of completeness for yourself around this line. Do not give the audience the impression that you are the guy with one line; rather, allow them to believe that your one line was all that needed to be said at that moment in time.

To have the confidence to direct

In this exercise you are asked to direct your own song. You may know that you never want to direct anything else in your life. What is important is that you get to experience the role of the director. You get to call the shots, make the decisions, and take responsibility for the end results. As Russell Grandstaff comments, "Your director assumes responsibility for everything that happens on the stage in front of the audience."[2] This is empowering for you as an actor, and it also gives you an appreciation for the role of the director. Some actors will comment that they are literally shoved in different directions while no attempt is made to garner their opinion. And yet, some of these same actors panic if a director even hints that they should come up with their own motivations. Do your homework on the scene and your character so that you can be prepared for any eventuality that comes up. Even if you feel like you are being treated like a puppet, you do not have to think like a puppet. Actors who are intelligent take decisive action to be so, and vice versa.

[2]Russell Grandstaff, *Acting and Directing* (Lincolnwood, IL: National Textbook Company, 1970), 30.

Chapter 14
Think Outside the Box

74. Object of Your Desire

Choose an object such as an apple and describe it. At first glance you might say the apple is red and round and hard. While this might be an accurate description of the apple, I want you to go a lot further. For instance, you could say the apple is a maroon red with a hint of lilac green, the texture is firm to touch and yet there is a mouthwatering softness beneath the surface. There are sparkling dewdrops rolling off all sides. There is a smell of sweetness likened to that of a rose wine from a fine bouquet. You could go on and on. Exhaust all possibilities. Try this with a number of different items. When I have done this activity with actors I often find they will be very literal at first glance. What we are looking for is as much detail as you can possibly give. If your mouth is not watering by the time you finish describing the apple, you still have a lot more describing to do.

Variables:

Continue this exercise in the world around you. How about looking up at the sky and describing the weather? Instead of saying it is a cloudy day, you could look at the sky and comment on the whispers of clouds that appear light and fluffy and foam-like in texture. Breaking through the clouds are streaks of aqua blue light that are engulfing and encapsulating everything around them. The cloud to the far left is brash and imposing, attempting to enforce its dullness on its surroundings and far reaching areas. The only limitations you have during this activity are the ones you put upon yourself.

Discussion:

What, in your opinion, is the purpose of this activity?

How did your perception of an item change once you had described it in detail?

Why does an actor need to be descriptive and articulate?

What breakthroughs or realizations did you make during this activity?

Purpose:

To utilize and expand your imagination

In this activity you get the opportunity to expand your imagination. When you first look at the apple, it is simply an apple. You have seen many before and perhaps think nothing of it. But when you describe its texture, its aroma, and its inner core, it is as if you are bringing the apple to life. As an actor, it is your responsibility to breathe life into whatever character you play. What if your character seems dull and lifeless and no information has been given to you? In the same way you were able to create an incredible amount of detail for the apple, you must now do this for each and every character you play. In discussing the topic of imagination, Napoleon Hill explains, "The sixth sense is creative imagination. The faculty of creative imagination is one which the majority of people never use during an entire lifetime, and if used at all, it usually happens by mere accident."[1] The actor is not in the position to allow this to happen by mere accident, but must do her utmost to create opportunities that encourage the expansion and growth of the imagination. By utilizing your imagination, you create new realities for yourself and believability for your audience.

To attempt to understand human nature

You may be wondering how looking at an apple could help you understand human nature. When you first looked at the apple, you had some preconceived notions as to what that apple was. Once you took the time to really go into detail, you found out a lot of new things that you had never considered before. Actors quite often fall into clichés with a character because they are too quick to assume. They create one-dimensional characters that do not exist in the real world. Let's say you have been cast as the girl working at the coffee shop and you want to make some bold choices. You decide that she must be pretty simple because otherwise why would she be working for minimum wage? What you may have forgotten to consider is that perhaps she is a third-year law student who works at the coffee shop to pay her way through school. Perhaps she is incredibly intelligent, articulate, and a stickler for order and detail. It is only when we are willing to delve beneath the surface that we can start to understand human nature. An actor who does not attempt to understand what motivates people is living in a bubble.

---

[1] Napoleon Hill, *Think and Grow Rich* (New York: Hawthorne Books, 1966), 205.

75. Matchbox Madness

This is an exercise that we were all asked to do in drama school many moons ago, and one that has quite famous origins. Take an ordinary matchbox, look at it, and write down every piece of detail related to the matchbox that you can come up with. When you are finished, look at and review your list. Here are some of the things you could have come up with (depending on your matchbox): it is made of thin cardboard, there are blue colors on each side rim, the top and bottom are colored in a bright red, each match is made of a wooden stick about one inch in length, and so on.

Repeat this exercise, and this time write down *everything* that you can conceivably imagine that relates to this matchbox. For example: if the matchbox is made of cardboard, then it is made of paper. If it is made of paper then it must come from a tree, if it comes from a tree then there must have been tree fellers to cut it down. They must have used an electric saw in order to do the job. The saw must have been powered from an electric battery. At some stage the battery was created from an energy source. The knowledge for that energy comes from science and the resources for science come from the universe. This is only a shortened version of how I want you to approach this exercise. Take a different object and follow the same procedure. You have just given yourself a new appreciation for something as simple as a matchbox.

Variables:
Come up with your own.

Discussion:
How has your view of the matchbox changed?
Did you find a new appreciation for objects? Explain your answer.
How did you utilize your imagination in this exercise?

Purpose:
To find a new appreciation for props
In this exercise you get to take an item as simple as a matchbox and appreciate how complex it is in its entirety. When you work with props, you need to give them a high level of respect. Let's say your character is nervous and on edge. This could be shown by the way you tap your fingers on your coffee cup, the way your fingers trace the surface of the rim, or the way you sip your coffee in short, fast, erratic bursts. Find a

new appreciation for your props because they are there to serve you and the scene and do not exist as a hindrance. In television, props are quite often not utilized enough because of continuity for filming, and yet the actors quite often look unsure as to what to do with their hands. Think about the amount of objects we hold in our hands or manipulate in some way throughout the day. Props are a great asset to you and can help further the story and action of the scene when utilized fully.

To expand your boundaries

When you first look at the matchbox, all you see is the matchbox. When you describe it, you can do so fairly methodically and mundanely. When you start to look at all the pieces that go into creating the matchbox, however, a whole new world opens up. You begin to realize the many cogs in the wheel that make the matchbox a possibility. You can use this way of thinking to break down a character's objectives and make more diverse choices. Let's say you are playing a bully who likes to beat up and tease weaker students. You might decide that this character is purely mean and that everything about him is hateful. You might believe he has no redeeming qualities and is a scourge on society. But what if you added the knowledge that his father beat him when he got home each night, and so becoming a bully was a learned and normal behavior? Deep down inside he wanted to be loved and feel part of a loving environment. By expanding your boundaries, you may find something new in the material that you hadn't seen at first. There are choices, there are good choices, and there are better choices.

76. Flicker Fantastic

This exercise involves an open flame, so please be cautious. Light a candle, preferably in the evening or at dusk. You can have a small amount of other light in the room, such as a lamp, but the candle should be the main source of light. Now stare directly into the flame. You should get fairly close, but keep it safe. As you stare into the flickering flame, make a mental note or write down whatever images come to you. For instance, as you look into the flame you might see a chariot driven by horses, or a tree blowing in the wind. Whatever images that flickering flame conjures up, make a note of them. See if you can come up with at least five. If you end up spending thirty minutes on one image, then you may stop there. However, you will most likely find that as the flame keeps on flickering, new images will come to you. If you are having trouble seeing images, you might want to squint your eyes slightly, which will give them a blurred sensation and probably make it easier for you to see images. Once you have finished, review your findings and blow out your candle.

Variables:
Use a lava lamp instead of a candle.

Discussion:
Did you find the flame to be mesmerizing or hypnotic in any sense?
At any point did you find you had to stop the activity to refocus?
What colors did you see within the flame?
What sparked your interest the most about this activity?

Purpose:
To utilize your imagination
This exercise allows you to explore your imagination as you explore the contents of the flame. You have already come across the term "imagination" several times in this book, and you will most likely come across it several more times. Having a creative imagination is an enormous part of what the actor does, and without it you may as well pack up your bag. The reason you see this term pop up again and again is because repetition is an excellent way of enhancing and developing your skills. Let's say you are working on a scene and a director asks you to try the scene again, only do it a different way this time. If you do not have a creative imagination, you are going to struggle here. Some directors will spoonfeed you, but hopefully you will also work with some quality directors who pull everything they possibly can from you. I want to make sure that when they start pulling, you have the ability and training to be able to give.

To create value
When you look at a flickering flame you normally see a flickering flame. Once you have completed this exercise, you will never see a flickering flame the same way again. This is a metaphor for the way you can start to observe life as an actor. As you go out and about on your daily travels, you can start to see the world around you as it relates to acting. Perhaps the tree that you walk past every day now reminds you of a character who is rather stiff. Perhaps the posture of the tree is one you can adapt for a certain character you might play in the future. In the

grocery store you might see a couple argue and then kiss and make up. This will allow you to see that human nature can be unpredictable and erratic. This information will help you to play against one-dimensional characters in your own work. While the classroom is a wonderful training ground for the actor, it is not the only one. Use the world around you to keep learning, growing, and expanding your horizons at every turn.

77. Dream Catcher

When you wake up first thing in the morning, try to review a dream you had during the night. As soon as you wake up, write down everything you can remember about your dream. You might not remember your dreams each night, so you are going to have to choose a morning that you remember your dream to work this activity. Some people do not dream or simply don't remember their dreams. If you fit into this category you can borrow a dream from one of your friends.

Take your dream and break it down into what you think it means. Let's say I dreamed I was walking into an amazing white mansion with beautiful high ceilings and stained-glass windows. The surroundings are lush and green with high trees and thick bushes. In the center of the living room is a cozy fireplace that is roaring with orange and red flames. There are two children in their pajamas playing with a toy bear, and in the kitchen I am making hot chocolate. The first thing I commented on was a white mansion. I might interpret this to mean that one day I will have great wealth. I said that the mansion was white so I am going to interpret this to mean my intentions are good and that I am not going to step on any toes along the way. In my dream I said the surroundings were lush and green with high trees. Perhaps the lush and green can be interpreted to say I am living a life that is full and creative. The tall trees could be an indication that I enjoy my privacy and like to be sheltered at times from distractions. I saw a cozy yet roaring fireplace. The cozy part may indicate my desire to have some comforts in my life and live a comfortable lifestyle. The roaring fire may be an indication that my mind is always roaring with ideas and that perhaps sometimes I need to slow down a little.

As I am sure you are aware, I made up everything you just read. Most likely you are not a dream expert either, and that is absolutely fine. Play with this exercise and see how you can interpret the information you are given. The most important part is that you look for the greater significance behind each thing that comes up for you. In other words, if you see a chair, it is not simply a chair; perhaps it signifies stability in your life. There are plenty of books on this topic at the library or bookstore that you can browse through if you want more knowledge to guide you. Once you are finished you can review your findings.

Variables:
Do you have some thoughts that are going around in your head? Look at these thoughts and see if you can work out the greater significance of their meaning.

Discussion:
How many attempts did it take you until you came up with a dream you could remember?

How long do you think you were dreaming for?

Was it fun to interpret your dream, or was it fairly draining?

Did you feel you learned anything new about yourself?

Purpose:
To encourage actors to keep on dreaming
When a person decides she wants to have a career as an actor, she is pursuing a dream. Everyone knows that acting is one of the most challenging professions in which to make a living. Many people will find their attempts to become actors are cut prematurely short for financial reasons or a whole slew of other reasons. Some individuals will give up because their agents don't get them work, or they get discouraged at auditions, or they are tired of the lifestyle they are living. Some people who love acting will give up their dream in high school when their teacher or parents tell them it is an unrealistic profession for them to get into. I am here to say keep on dreaming! Leo Buscaglia quotes Herbert Otto when he says, "'We are all functioning at a small fraction of our capacity to live fully in its total meaning of loving, caring, creating, and adventuring. Consequently, the actualizing of our potential can become the most exciting adventure of a lifetime.'"[2] If you are willing to work hard for the rest of your life, have a thick skin, have an enormous amount of drive, have other reasons for acting outside of fame and fortune, have some sort of game plan to make your dreams a reality, and are willing to keep going when the going gets tough, you have what it takes. If you really believe that this is the career for you and there is

[2]Leo Buscaglia, *Love* (New York: Ballantine Books, 1982), 43.

nothing else you want to do with your life, then do it. No one can steal your dreams from you except you.

To look for the hidden meaning

If you took your dream literally, it may be a fun little story and nothing more. We are often told that our dreams are the wants, desires, and fears that make up who we are. If the tall trees in my hypothetical dream meant I enjoyed my privacy, then this is useful information for me to have. In your acting, your character will have words that you might choose to take very literally. For example, "I didn't work today because I felt sick." If we take this at face value then it works fine. But what if your character didn't work today because he simply wanted to stay at home and watch football? He has just told a lie that may need to come out in the subtext of what you are saying. Our dreams have hidden meanings and so does a lot of what people (and characters) say. If you have a thorough understanding of your character and the play/movie, you will have a better understanding to drive the subtext of what you are saying. Some actors may have only one line in a movie, so they decide to learn their one line and not read the rest of the script. This is a big mistake, as there are other pieces of information that might be very useful to you. Do your homework, go the extra mile, and grab as much as you possibly can.

78. Trail Blazing

For this activity you are going to get to do some exercise, so I trust you are feeling energetic. Near my home in Los Angeles we have a beautiful place to walk called Runyon Canyon. It climbs around and through the beautiful hills of L.A., giving you a panoramic view. If you keep going up, then eventually you will start coming down. On the way down it can be a little tricky in parts, and there are a number of options on how to go down each little gradient. Sometimes there are a number of paths to go down the same area, but often it is simply where you place your footing that can change every time. Of course this can also apply to climbing up the canyon.

Find a nature trail, canyon, or hill near where you live and go explore. Go back on more than one occasion and see if you can find different paths or different avenues to take the same trail. Perhaps it is simply your foot placement on tricky parts of the trail that changes. Perhaps the more times you go, the more paths you discover. I am not asking you to take dangerous risks and create paths that are not there. Safety must always come first. This is an activity you can do time and time again. Enjoy the view and your surroundings and pay attention to how you begin to negotiate that trail slightly differently each time you go. Notice how you never walk the path exactly the same way on any two occasions.

Variables:

Walk the trail very early in the morning and then very late in the evening and see if this changes the way you negotiate the trail.

Discussion:

Were you surprised at how many different ways you could negotiate the trail?

Did you begin to find ways down that you didn't even know were there?

Did you notice things on the trail that you hadn't seen on other occasions?

As an actor, what is the benefit of putting fresh air in your lungs?

Purpose:

**To realize there are many potential paths
on your journey as an actor**

When you negotiate difficult parts of your trail you have to be sure of your footing. As you continue further, you may have to adjust your footing to somewhere you had not at first considered in order to keep yourself from slipping. You can have ideas in mind of where to place your feet, but, if needed, you are flexible enough to change them at the last moment.

This is a metaphor for your acting journey. You may have all these pre-conceived ideas of how you are going to become famous and how you are going to never be out of work. You have an exact plan, and you are going to stick to it. I admire the fact that you have a plan — that is more than most people have — but, unfortunately, it may not be enough. You have to be willing to change, adapt, and mold your plan as you go. If something is not working for you, do not continue to bash your head against a brick wall. Let's say that you were trained at a wonderful school with a very prestigious reputation. Some years down the road, you get offered a daytime soap that is going to pay very well. You think about your training and remember that you were taught to only do work of integrity. You turn down the soap so that you can keep your integrity as an actor. If you can afford to do this and have enough other acting work to keep you going, then fine. If not, take the soap! How many actors can say they earn good money acting? By taking the soap, you are not giving up on your ideals; rather, you are giving yourself the opportunity to work as an actor and, as a result, you'll have more financial security to search for the projects you really want down the road. When you had to keep from falling, or simply to find out what it was like, you adapted the way you negotiated your trail. Be willing and able to do the same thing for your acting journey. When talking about boys who survived the Holocaust, Martin Gilbert says, "The memories which the boys guard are among the last living testimonies to the Jewish world of those towns, fifty-five years after that world was destroyed forever."[3] No matter what the challenges of life, no matter how devastating, one must always find the path and find a way to move forward with life. If you put your life in perspective as an actor, you are far more fortunate then many in being given an opportunity to follow your dreams.

To be in and around nature

You may be thinking that this sounds very wishy-washy, but think again. Being in nature can be very grounding for the actor — or for anyone, for that matter. If you live in a large city, you are most likely surrounded by a lot of things that are fake and plastic. Nature, on the other hand, is very real and very true. Not only is nature centering, it is wonderful for clearing the mind. As an actor you want to create the full potential for creativity in your life. If, as an actor, you can live in a creative state, then your imagination and drive can become boundless. You are also training your mental muscles to live in a creative state so that it becomes second nature to you. Integrating nature into your life is a leap in this direction.

79. Water Works

For this exercise you are going to want to find some water. The swimming pool, the ocean, and a lake are a few possibilities. You are also going to need a bathing suit, some goggles, and, if possible, some

---

[3]Martin Gilbert, *The Boys* (London: The Guernsey Press Co., 1996), 5.

snorkeling equipment or even diving gear. Go under the water, and as you swim around think about the environment you are in. Notice how different you feel from your known environment. Notice how your body starts to regulate itself in a different way. As your sense of hearing adjusts, how does this adjust your overall state? Notice if you are experiencing a feeling of inner peace or feeling somewhat freer than usual. Obviously, come up for air as often as you need to. To stay under longer, you can use one of those cheap snorkels for the swimming pool. If you are going to the ocean and have diving gear, that's even better.

As you are swimming around, think about acting. I don't want to tell you what to think about acting, just think about acting. When you think about acting in this environment, in this frame of mind, you may find some interesting results. Perhaps you could run through the words of a scene you are currently working on. Maybe you could run some visual images of a play you are presently performing in. Whatever you do, I want you to make sure it is all happening under the water. Perhaps you are just thinking about the world of acting and what it means to you. Perhaps you are thinking about how far you have come over the years as you have grown as an actor. Perhaps you are thinking about the fact that there is truly nothing else you would rather be doing with your life. As I said, you are free to think about anything you want as long as it is related to acting. When you are finished, get in a nice hot shower and dry off with a big fluffy towel.

Variables:

If you want to take this to a different level, as you go under water, close your eyes as well. I would suggest if you are going to do this you might want to stay a little more static rather than crash into all and sundry.

Discussion:

How does being underwater heighten your sense of awareness?
Was your thinking clearer or more clouded under the water?
Is there anything calming about being underwater?
What was your impression of the sounds and noises around you?

Purpose:

To influence your thinking in a kinesthetic manner

The title above sounds pretty intellectual, doesn't it? It simply means that by changing your environment we can change the way our body and mind interprets. By going underwater, you get to experience this at a physiological level. Now, this exercise is not an exact science, and so you might say that your thinking patterns were exactly the same as normal. You might say that your imagination was not affected in any way. My hypothesis is that you will find a change in your imagination and thinking patterns during this exercise. It is also worth noting that acting is not an exact science, and what works for one actor might work differently for another. When you are on a set that is supposed to be below zero and you have powerful lights shining in your face and you are sweating profusely, it is your imagination that will be your ally. But imagination alone is not enough. You are going to have to find the absolute depths of cold at a physiological level. You are going to have to put this into your body at a kinesthetic level. Those powerful lights that are burning you up are actually sending chills down your spine, or so the actor creates.

To get you to think about acting everywhere

When most people go to the ocean or the swimming pool, the last thing on their mind is acting. This is unless they are in the middle of filming a scene when the last thing on their mind should be acting. In the middle of the pool/ocean/lake I am asking you to think about acting, acting, acting. I want you to make observations, make discoveries, and/or rekindle your passion for acting. Being an actor is one thing, and being passionate about acting is totally different. Under the water is a good place to think about acting because under these circumstances you might come up with new ideas. By changing your environment, your shift and focus may totally change. Perhaps you have been thinking about how you need to shift your acting career but are not sure how. By shifting your environment and being under the water, perhaps the answers will come to you. Sounds a little far-fetched and crazy, doesn't it? But then, so does a career in acting.

80. Plant the Seed

For this exercise I would like you to find an open space. Curl yourself up into a ball as if you were a tiny seed. Close your eyes to allow yourself to fully utilize your imagination. Imagine that the roots of the seed are growing firmly into the ground and making a solid foundation. As you start to grow, decide what you are growing into. Perhaps you are a flower or a plant or even a banana tree. Start to grow slowly and continue to expand. Imagine now that you are on an island such as Haiti or Hawaii and that there are strong winds gusting through. As the winds gust through, hold your ground even if you start to sway from side to side. The winds get stronger and stronger and fiercer and fiercer. They have now become a strong hurricane and are threatening to rip you from the ground. No matter how strong the winds get, you have to stay as firm as the roots that are firmly planted in the ground. You have to hold on for dear life and not give in. After a length of time the winds subside and you know you have survived the storm. Continue to grow, continue to expand until you are fully matured. Now you can feel the sun and its rays gliding over you and giving you life energy. Think of how far you have come from being a small, tiny seed to what you are today.

Variables:

Instead of being in a hurricane perhaps you could be in a snowstorm or a vicious hailstorm.

Discussion:

How did you manage to hold your ground when the hurricane became a force to reckon with?

Did you feel your roots going into the ground?

What is the significance of starting out as a small seed?

Did closing your eyes enhance your imagination in any way?

Purpose:

To create a metaphor for your acting career

In this exercise you are asked to start as a small seed with roots in the ground. In some way this is comparable to your acting career. You start out as a small seed and plant your roots firmly in the ground. Your roots are your training, your acting, your discipline, your professionalism, your organizational skills, your desire to understand and explore the craft of acting, and your desire to understand the ropes of the industry you are entering. In this activity you were asked to stand firm even when engulfed by a hurricane. At some point, your acting career is going to feel a little bit like this. You are going to feel like you are being hit from every direction and that you do not know which way to turn. You need to pay your bills, your agent isn't calling, you've had no auditions, your car needs to be fixed, your headshot doesn't work, and you have to find another job. There will be many times like these in your acting career and you will have to be strong enough to weather the storm. If you don't have your roots deeply planted in the soil, you are going to be swept away. Obviously, this is a metaphor, but go to any of the big acting hubs and you will find that what I am saying is a reality. If you are able to weather the storm, you will have grown stronger and learned many lessons along the way. You will have become tougher and more streetwise, and, with luck and tenacity, you will have carved out a place for yourself as a working actor. There are many different avenues you can take as an actor that can help you achieve your goals. Actors are known to direct, instruct, write, or produce, to name but a few areas. Be creative about your approach and be willing to have different fires burning simultaneously.

Connecting the imagination to the physical body

In this exercise you are asked to close your eyes to bring your attention to your imagination. As you grow from a seed into a plant/tree, you are physically changing. In order for you to believe those physical changes, you are going to have to use the aid of your imagination. Without your imagination you will simply be going through the steps. The imagination is the gel that connects the physical to the mental and the mental to the physical. It is the imagination that unleashes the actors' playground. If you want to know how this is relevant to your career as an actor, go to any audition, and you will find that ninety percent of the actors lack imagination. These are not my words, but those of a casting director. It means that while the actors may understand the piece technically, they don't have the foggiest idea what it's about. They are unable to bring something that has not been given to them. What if you have to do the same scene for thirty takes? What if you are performing in the same play for two years? A friend of mine told me that Yul Brenner played the part of the King of Siam in *The King and I* for twenty-seven years. Can you imagine playing the same role for twenty-seven years? In order for him to have audiences flocking to see him for this amount of time, he must have kept the part alive and fresh through his creative imagination.

Chapter 15
Characterization

81. Bio Monolog

Part one

Start this exercise by finding a day when you can set aside a minimum of four hours. Go to a crowded place with a high volume of people such as a shopping mall, a crowded street, or a busy park. At first glance what I want you to do may seem unethical, so I will ask you to do it in the most unobtrusive manner possible. As actors, we are always stretching the boundaries in some fashion or other. Your task is to seek out an individual (a total stranger) and spend a minimum of one hour in observation of him or her. I want you to literally follow someone around for one hour. If you are male, I prefer you follow a man and vice versa. I suggest you choose someone who intrigues you in some way; the reason for this will be revealed in a moment.

So why, you ask, do you need to put aside a minimum of four hours? If you have ever tried to follow someone around for a whole hour, you will find it is easier said than done. I have found that it is quite easy to lose people or come close to being discovered. (By the way, if you find that a person becomes suspicious, this is probably the time to move on to someone else or start practicing your acting skills.) Four hours is about the average amount of time needed to complete this exercise.

As you follow your chosen person around, take notes: how does she move, how does she walk, how does she sit, how does she speak, how does she eat, laugh, frown, wipe her face, etc.? At no point should you strike up a conversation or sit in too close a proximity so that she becomes aware of your presence. The idea is to be a fly on the wall, not a hawk. Maintain some ethical boundaries. If she goes into a changing room, do not follow her in. Make your notes as specific as possible, and even if you observe something of minute detail, write it down. When your hour is up and you feel you have enough information, part one is complete. If you decide to stay with the same person for longer than an hour, that's fine. Take the information you have written, read over it, review it, let it sink in, and put it in a safe place.

Part two

Wait about twenty-four hours before starting this second section. Retrieve and review your notes. Perhaps you found that the person was left handed, crossed her legs when she sat down, had a habit of scratching her chin on a regular basis, had a shrill laugh, and so on. Now I want you to make some bold assumptions about this person. What is her job? Is she married or single? How many children does she have? How old is she? What neighborhood does she live in? How does she react in high-pressure situations? Use your notes and your imagination to develop this section. Come up with as many questions and answers as you feel are necessary until you feel you have a good understanding of who this individual really is. Make sure your answers are as specific as possible. If you decided that this lady was a secretary, then write down what type of secretary. Is she a legal secretary, is she a secretary at a local car showroom, is she a senior or entry-level secretary? How many words can she type per minute? In your answers, move as far away from generalities as possible. When you feel you have enough information, put it in a safe place and let everything you wrote sink in for the next twenty-four hours.

Part three

After twenty-four hours, take out your notes and review them once again. Next comes a new and exciting challenge for you. Write a monolog for your chosen person based on your notes and observations. The monolog should be about one to two minutes in length, and it should really let us get to know this person. Don't write what I would call an exposition monolog, where you literally give us the information. For instance, "I am twenty-four years old, and yesterday I got divorced, and I lost my job at the supermarket." This is throwing information at us in a hurry for the sake of getting the information across. Write a monolog that sums up who this person really is: "I like to come here early in the morning. I like the silence. I like the fact that I don't have to deal with all that hustle and bustle." We get a real flavor of the individual without being bombarded with sterile facts. Remember, you originally chose a person that intrigued you in some way. This is where it pays off. The more interesting you find the person, the more your monolog will come alive. Give yourself a one-hour time limit in which to write your monolog. This piece is going to be for your own exploration, so it does not have to be a masterpiece. Once you have your monolog, read through it a couple of times and let it sink in. Put your monolog in a safe place and do not come back to it for about twenty-four hours.

Part four

In your own time, learn your monolog and perform it. Some people like to learn the lines first and others like to learn them as they explore.

Do what is right for you. Be the director of your own monolog — you make the choices and decisions. Come up with your own blocking, motivation, and justifications. If you so decide, you can come up with a costume to complement your character. Explore this piece as often as you like and take it in as many different directions as you can. You may choose to involve props if you feel they will complement the scene. If you decide you want to repeat this exercise by following a different person, wait at least a month before starting the process again. This will allow enough time for everything you have discovered to sink in so that you can make a clean break. Please do not get carried away by intruding on this individual's life — keep your boundaries and your integrity at all times.

Variables:

Instead of following a person around you could study a picture in a magazine. You could then create your character's background and monolog simply by using the still picture in front of you as a basis from which to begin. Use the same process as before and see the exercise through in its entirety.

Discussion:

What were the choices you made in performing your monolog?

Did you create the essence of the person you chose, or did you end up with a caricature?

What was the hardest part of the exercise?

If you did this activity again, how might you do it differently?

What difference to you did it make that your monolog was based on a real person and not a make-believe one?

Purpose:

To create real life from real life

Most of the characters you will play throughout your career will not be based on real people. Some actors find it difficult to play reality when they perceive their character as false or fake. This is an enormous error and will actually take away from the believability in your work. This exercise will help you shift gears and realize that you have to see each character you play as real, regardless of the material you are given to begin with. You are going out into the real world to observe real people. You cannot get any more real than that. If the character is not real for you, then how do you expect the audience to see him that way?

To experience the discovery process in stages

What if I had given you this exercise, asked you to observe someone, and left it at that? It would still have been pretty rewarding, but perhaps would have stopped far short of the full potential. By taking this activity one step at a time, you are able to add a new phase of understanding with each step. In the rehearsal process, the actor should also be willing to take the necessary steps to enable the potential for constant discovery. Say you are in a scene and your fellow actor says he doesn't want to rehearse the scene, but would rather fly it by the seat of his pants. Go through the steps anyway and make your own discoveries; rehearse the scene by yourself if you have to — at least you will be prepared even if your fellow actor is not. You can only truly take responsibility for yourself. As much as you may want to take ownership for someone else, you cannot. Acting is a process that takes many stages to get to the end result. Skip through the stages and it will show in your work. You don't have to take my word for it; turn on your television and decide for yourself how many actors are skipping and skimming through their preparation.

82. Age Awareness

This is an exercise I have seen used on different occasions. In 1996 I took a financial seminar and they had us tie our feet and our hands together to make the connection between this physical bind and the financial bind many people find themselves in. I have adapted this exercise for the actor to experience what it feels like to physically grow old.

Take a piece of clothesline, rope, or anything that is not too abrasive. Now tie your feet together (not too tight), then take the same piece of rope and, bringing it between your legs from the posterior side of your body, throw the rope over your left or right shoulder, and tie it to your feet once more. It should not be too tight, but it should be tight enough that you are slightly hunched over and have restricted movements. What you have just done in a matter of minutes is create the sensation of scoliosis of the spine. Instead of simply moving as an older person, you now have real and tangible restrictions on your body that allow you to experience what it can be like to grow old. You also have restricted movement in your feet and will most likely find you have to shuffle around as opposed to taking strides. Now, just as in a number of other exercises in this book, I want you to complete a number of tasks of your choice in this manner. Go make your bed, do the laundry, or type a letter at your computer. It is important that you do not adjust the rope to ease your restrictions. I want you to get the full experience of finding ways to cope with these new physical challenges. I want to make it clear that the aim is not to cut off your circulation. Always remember to work smart.

Variables:

See if you can come up with your own by utilizing your imagination.

Discussion:

How did the physical restraints imposed on you further your understanding of growing old?

In what way do you think it was important to experience this activity in a kinesthetic sense as opposed to simply discussing it in a theoretical sense?

In what part of your body did you notice change first? How did that affect your movement?

How did this activity allow you to become more aware of your body?

Purpose:

To solve challenges

During this activity you will constantly be dealing with and learning to adjust to the challenges that face you. Let's say you need to bend down to tie your shoelace. Your newfound restrictions are going to make this somewhat difficult. You are going to have to find new and imaginative ways to tie your shoe. With each challenge you solve, you will find yourself presented with a new challenge.

You will constantly be presented with challenges in your acting that you will need to solve. Let's say when you are looking over the script for an audition, you realize that the script is very weak and that there seems to be no justification for what your character says. It is up to you to solve the challenge in front of you. Find a justification for why your character might say these things. Make bold choices and commit to your choices during your audition. Do not turn yourself into a puppet that can only move when its strings are being pulled. Empower yourself to take charge of your acting choices rather than waiting for someone else to do it for you.

To experience your character's center of gravity

A person's center of gravity is the point of origin in their body that leads their movement. While it is quite possible to have a combination of more than one area, one body part is usually more dominant. With the rope restricting your movements, you are probably going to find that you lead with your head. You will probably notice that your neck is also jutting forward and this affects the rest of your body. We can say that your center of gravity is one you will create in an external sense. In other words, it is a physical positioning of the body that you could manipulate and change depending on the character you are playing. Try leading with your knees, shoulders, pelvis, or chest and see how different you feel. What is also important to note is that as your physicality changes, so do your internal reactions. Not only will your body feel different internally, you will also find that your personality is affected. As Moni Yakim explains, "This awareness must have an effect on you."[1] In one instance you may feel more confident, but leading with a different center you may find yourself feeling more shy and withdrawn.

83. Outfit Awareness

For this exercise, you get to play dress up. Well, this is only a half-truth. What I would like you to do is go against the grain of how you normally like to dress. Perhaps your friends always comment on how smartly you dress, so to today you dress scruffy. Put on that old, dirty pair of jeans and the scraggy t-shirt. Go one step further and neglect your hair and teeth if you are going for a scruffy look.

For the next part of this exercise, go to a mall or another busy place where you are likely to come across large amounts of people. Go into a clothing store and ask some questions about an outfit. See what kind of reactions you get and whether the person you are talking to is giving off a friendly vibe or something totally different. By the way, you are only being asked to change your clothing, not yourself. You should not do anything to differentiate your personality from the way you normally are. The only thing you are being asked to change about yourself is your appearance. Go into one or two other shops, ask some questions, and see how the employees respond to you. Are you being greeted politely, or are people more defensive and standoffish? See what reactions you

[1]Moni Yakim, *Creating a Character* (New York: Watson-Guptill Publications, 1990), 27.

get from other people, as well. Do people walk close, or do they appear to be moving further away from you? Make some notes on your discoveries.

Go back to the mall on another occasion and in a contrasting outfit. Perhaps this time you could dress very smart and then proceed with the activity in exactly the same way. You may want to experiment by going to the same shops and speaking to exactly the same people. Do you find as you are walking around that people seem to be giving you more respect? Make notes of your discoveries and what you are finding. You do not have to use scruffy/smart; you can choose whatever you want. As a reminder, you are not playing a character but keeping your own personality the whole time. It is interesting for actors to discover firsthand the power of costumes and how it will affect the way people respond and interact with you. You do not have to go to the mall, but I ask you to use caution and choose a safe environment. I suggest talking to shop assistants because this is safe and because it is their job to talk with you and help you as a member of the public.

Variables:

Instead of changing your clothing, give yourself an impediment such as a lisp or a slight eye squint (such as with a person who needs glasses). This is not to make fun of people with impediments, but rather to highlight the way you are perceived and treated by members of the public. I do not want you to exaggerate, but take a subtle approach to whatever you choose. Make notes about your discoveries and explore what you find.

Discussion:

What was the most surprising reaction or comment you received?

How did this activity highlight the importance of costumes and the actor?

What assumptions did you perceive people were making about you on each separate occasion?

If Hollywood perceives actors as a product, how does clothing play into this?

Purpose:

Characterization

There is a common saying that reads, "Clothes make the man," and to some degree I think we can say, "The costume makes the character."

The clothing that we wear tells people something about us. In this activity you experienced people making assumptions about you based on what you were wearing. Can you imagine playing a character who wears high heels as opposed to one who walks around barefoot? The difference will have an enormous influence on the way you interpret this character and also on the way you move as this character. I have heard it said that costumes are unimportant for a character, but I beg to differ. Whether we like it or not, people will make assumptions about us based on the way we are dressed, and this could, at the very least, influence the dynamics of a scene.

To understand clothing in relation to the audition process

In this activity, the importance of clothing is highlighted. In the audition process your attention to detail in your choice of clothing is just as important. Let's say you are auditioning for the role of a police officer. You turn up in jeans and a ripped t-shirt and are surprised when you don't get a callback. The impression you probably made was of someone who could not even be bothered to make the slightest effort to find the character. This may not be true, but it is most likely what was perceived. Let's say you got called on another audition, and this time it was for a nurse character. You remembered what happened last time, so this time you went full out and bought a nurse's uniform complete with a clip on watch. After the audition you waited patiently and still didn't get a callback. You couldn't for the life of you understand what went wrong. I would suggest that this time you went too far in your costuming and that for the audition process all you need is something that suggests the character. For the police officer, perhaps you could have worn something a little more formal, such as a button down shirt. For the nurse, you may have wanted to wear soft, warm colors that suggest a warm and nurturing person. There are so many factors that determine whether or not you get the part, so let's not make your clothing or costume a factor to work against you.

84. *Aprender Idioma*

For this exercise, choose a language that you would like to learn. Let's say you have always had the desire to learn French — now is your opportunity. I don't expect you to learn your language of choice fluently, but if this happened it would be a bonus. The aim is to explore and pick up as much as you can.

Over the next eight weeks, become familiar with this language. Let's say I chose to learn French. I might decide to read a basic how-to book in French. I might listen to music in French and rent movies that are in French with English subtitles. As I am driving in the car, I might put my radio on a French language station. I may decide to visit a French café. Perhaps I could join a French club to talk with others or even sign up for a basic French course. Down the road I might even decide to take a trip to France. I don't want to tell you how much to do each day; I will leave this entirely up to you. At the end of eight weeks you may find you are enjoying this new language so much that you want to continue learning and growing; please feel free to do so.

Variables:
Refer to exercise 39: Dialectician (page 80).

Discussion:
What extra resources could you use to help learn the language you chose?

Did you dedicate enough time to really take advantage of this exercise?

Were you surprised at how much you learned in eight weeks?

What learning apparatus are you using that parallels to that in your acting?

Purpose:
To broaden your range of communication
In this activity you are learning to communicate in a totally foreign language even if you are not doing it with great style. If you keep going, then eventually you will become fluent in your language of choice. As an actor, you are being asked to communicate a story on a regular basis. Communicating with your audience is a necessity. I'm not saying you should be able to speak another language, but can you imagine the potential in your acting work if you could? Acquiring more skills to communicate your message can only lead to enhance your work. One of the exciting things about learning a language is that you have to make an extra-concentrated effort to communicate with others. You may speak slowly at first and put all your effort into your desire to be understood. This exercise reminds the actor that it is his desire to be understood, to communicate, and to tell the story that will drive the piece.

To develop your learning abilities

In this exercise you are utilizing your learning abilities in many ways. You are using your memorization to learn words and sentences. You use different techniques to take the words off the page and formulate them as your own. For instance, when you actually start to go out and talk to people, you are using a very effective technique for learning a language. You do not just learn the words but also need to form an understanding of what they mean and how they can be used. All of these skills apply to acting in much the same way. An actor needs to excel as far as memorization is concerned. This applies to learning your lines but also to blocking, recalling previously given notes by the director, and so on. The word "technique" is a loaded one in the acting world. You will often be asked, "What technique do you practice?" This means, "Are you using Meisner, Stanislavski, Grotowski, Strasberg, Adler, or a different technique?" I would recommend that you explore as many techniques as you can throughout your acting career. The only word of caution I would raise is this if you study Meisner for two weeks, you cannot say you are trained in or understand Meisner. You will have to thoroughly understand a technique before you can really lay judgment to it. It is also worth noting that if you study the Strasberg technique, you are not really studying pure Strasberg technique. The reason I say this is because the only person who taught pure Strasberg technique was Lee Strasberg himself. It was his intuition that defined his work, so unless you are him, you cannot really teach his work purely. I say this as a word of caution for when you are deciding with whom to study. Know what you want to gain from the training and what your expectations are.

85. Stronger and Stronger

For this exercise, put your thinking cap on. Come up with a weak statement — a generalized statement. An example would be, "I want something to drink." Take this statement and make it into a stronger and clearer statement. An example would be, "I want a cup of coffee, please." This is much more specific and tells us exactly what you want. Another example of a weak statement would be, "I will try to meet you there sometime later." A stronger statement would be, "I will meet you at Bingos restaurant at four PM on Thursday." Come up with your own list of ten weak statements and turn each of them into clear and specific statements. As a reminder, a weak statement is more general with no clear direction. A stronger statement will be more specific with clear objectives.

Variables:

It may be interesting to listen to your friends or people you meet when you're out and about and see if they are making weak statements or strong, clear ones. You do not need to comment on this to them, but make mental notes of your observations and findings.

Discussion:

How did you come up with the criteria for a strong statement?

How often do you find yourself and others using weak statements in your day-to-day life?

Why is being clear and specific important for you as an actor?

How will using strong and clear language at an audition benefit you?

Purpose:

To enhance your chances at an audition

In this exercise you are asked to make very strong, clear, and specific choices. By the end of your sentence we should know exactly what you mean and exactly what you want. When you go for a professional audition, there is no time to be wishy-washy. No one is trying to strike up an in-depth conversation with you; they just want to get to the facts. If you are asked, "Where are you from?" Then you are expected to give a straightforward answer: "I'm from Denver, Colorado." You do not need to give your whole life history at this point. Some actors believe the more they talk the better chance they will have, while in fact the opposite is true. Can you imagine a day in which the casting director has to audition one hundred and fifty people? Do you really think he has time for small talk and vague answers? It is up to you to sell yourself at the audition and be professional in every sense of the word. If you don't like the sound of being professional, then go get another profession because you won't last five minutes in this one.

To guide you in creating a character background

I have asked you to accept the idea for the purpose of this activity that a vague statement is a weak one. Think about being given a script — let's say it's a script for a "short" or a student film. You will quite often find the character breakdown says something like this: "John is in his twenties, white, gets angry a lot." Please do not hunt me down if you are a writer of student films; I am obviously generalizing, but I have seen many scripts with breakdowns such as this. If this is all you are given, then it is up to you to create a background for your character. Let's say you accepted the idea that your character is twenty-something; this is a very weak statement. Have you ever met anyone in your life that is twenty-something? Now create your own clear and strong statement such as, "I am twenty-four years old, and my birthday is on November fourth." The character will automatically start to become more real to you. What if the script tells you that your name is Tom? This again is a vague statement, and you would do well to create a last name for your character such as Tom Edwards. Be aware that some directors might take offense to your background work and so there is no need to share it with them if you do not feel it is necessary. The idea of creating a clear and concise character background is to help you as an actor. Constantin Stanislavski said, "Any role that does not include a real characterization will be poor, not lifelike, and the actor who cannot convey the character of the roles he plays is a poor and monotonous actor."[2] Every role is different, and it is up to you to find out why.

---

[2]Constantin Stanislavski, *An Actor's Handbook* (New York: Theatre Art Books, 1994), 33.

Chapter 16
Improvisation

86. Frenzy

Have you ever woken up in the morning late for work and realized that you could not find your keys? For this exercise, reenact the scene of looking for your keys. Actually hide your own keys somewhere (of course you will know where they are) and then go through a scene of looking everywhere to find them. Be careful with this exercise — it sounds easy when in fact it is not. I will often see actors pretend to lift up a towel or pretend to look in a cupboard. If you're going to look in the cupboard, really look in the cupboard! In everything you do it must be clear that finding these keys is imperative to you.

Take a break and then work this activity again, this time building a background for your character. How old are you? What is your job? How late are you? Do you live alone or with someone else? Is this a stressful situation for you? How do you act under stress? What is your favorite color? Spend at least ten minutes developing your character and the situation before repeating the scene. Note how your results differ from the first time now that you have this extra information.

When you are finished I would like you to take a few minutes and make a few more notes. Repeat the exercise again, and this time, really "raise the stakes." Have a very important reason why you must find your keys immediately. Perhaps if you are late for work one more time you will lose your job, and you know that if you lose your job you will not be able to meet your car payments, so you will lose your car. You also realize that you will not be able to meet your mortgage payments, so you will lose your house. Suddenly the importance level of finding your keys has soared. When you work this scene for the third time, instead of hiding actual keys, use your imagination. If you think of the importance of the scene this time, there might be a degree of irrationality in the way you are searching. Think about all the things that are going to happen if you fail to find your keys. "Normal people" sometimes act in the most irrational ways in certain situations. I am not asking you to act irrational, but I am saying that there is a possibility that to a greater or lesser degree, irrationality may find its way into your scene. You do not have to use the job scenario that I gave you. Come up with your own as long as it has great importance attached to it. Once you are finished, let everything that has happened sink in: if you are not sweating at this point then you were holding back.

Don't lose your keys!

Variables:

Use the same sense of urgency, but instead of losing your keys perhaps you could be at a bus stop waiting for your bus, which is late. Instead of losing something, use an event to trigger the sense of urgency.

Discussion:

At what point were you really looking for the keys, and at what point were you simply going through the motions of pretending to look?

Did you stay in one room or look in different places?

Did you go back and look in the same place again or only go to each place one time?

What feelings were going through your body the moment you found your keys?

Purpose:

To commit to the action

I mentioned that it is quite common to see an actor pretend to look under a chair or pretend to look in a drawer. In this activity you are asked to actually look in the drawer or really move the chair. The challenge for some actors is that they know the keys are not under the chair so they don't make any real effort to look, and yet they must. If you don't commit to the action, you are wasting your time. You often hear people say that in life it is the journey that is important and not the goal. In terms of your audience, it will be far more interesting to watch you search for the keys than when you actually find them. Think how many times you have seen a play or movie where the actor has failed to commit to the action; I hope you are not one of those actors.

To understand the concept of raising the stakes

When you performed the scene for the first time, perhaps you did not have a great deal of importance attached to the scene. Maybe you told yourself, "I have to find the keys or I will be late." You see how this is very general and has no real meaning. When you were asked to make stronger and more important choices, suddenly the degree of importance attached to finding the keys was intensified. That intensity in your acting will permeate right through your work to your audience. Raising the stakes is another useful technique to add to your toolbox, even though every scene you are in will not necessarily require it. You may have a director who tells you that you need to speed a scene up.

178

This is bad direction, but if this is what you are given, then this is what you have to work with. Perhaps at this point you might use raising the stakes to help you find the justification for the scene to become intensified. If you simply choose to speed up because this is what you were asked to do, then that is exactly what will come across to your audience — a fast scene without any justification.

87. Urgency Build Up

This is an exercise that I was given in drama school that I have used on many occasions with actors. Act out (pantomime) the following short improvisation in your living room: Imagine you are in your home preparing for your vacation. You are getting out of bed and getting dressed. Please remember to put on your shoes and tie your laces. Brush your teeth, comb your hair, make a bowl of cereal, eat your bowl of cereal, open your suitcase, check that you have everything in it, and close your suitcase. Now pick up your imaginary suitcase, open your front door, go out your door, close your door, and lock your door. Head to the train station. (Instead of walking from one side of your living room to the other, walk in a figure-eight pattern to create the idea of distance and space.) As you arrive at the train station, check the timetable and, using your finger, find the time of your particular train. Go to the ticket window and buy your ticket for the train, then go to the platform, wait for your train, and get on your train as it arrives.

Take seven minutes to complete the entire exercise. Do not take three minutes or twelve minutes or five minutes. Wear a stopwatch or set an alarm clock. Do not make looking at your watch/clock the focus of the activity, but be aware that you must utilize your seven-minute time limit. When you are finished, take in what you just performed and bring yourself back to a place of neutrality.

Now repeat the exercise, this time with a time-limit of three minutes. You are still catching the train for your vacation, and you still need to complete all of your tasks. The only difference is your time limit. Please do not skim or skip any of the tasks. You are going to need a new sense of urgency and determination this time. When you are finished, take a short pause to contrast your experiences between the first and second time. I would like you to take a moment to bring yourself back to homeostasis as you are about to go for a third time.

This time, complete all the tasks in forty-five seconds. Again, it is important for you to remember that you cannot skim over any of the tasks. There is going to be an extreme sense of urgency for you to catch your train on time. It is quite possible that you will miss your train; however, you have to do everything in your power to catch it. When you are finished, review and contrast the three experiences.

Variables:

Instead of catching a train, come up with other alternatives for which time can become a factor.

Discussion:

What was going through your mind when you had seven minutes to catch your train?

When you realized that you only had forty-five seconds to get everything done, did you ever believe you could catch your train? Explore your answer fully and decide how this is relevant to the rest of your acting.

How does timing have the potential to play a vital role in a character's journey?

Purpose:

Understanding the role of time

In this exercise you are asked to perform the same scene in three different ways. The only part that is changed for you is the length of time, yet the scene is profoundly different because of this fact. Sometimes when you are working with a director he will tell you to "go quicker." This is bad direction, as it says nothing of motivation for your actions. You will then have to create the motivation for yourself in a similar fashion to the one used in this activity. By using a justified sense of urgency you are able to speed up the scene effectively. This exercise allows you to appreciate the importance of understanding the pacing of a scene. If your scene is rushed, it will have specific meaning to the audience. Everything you say or do in a scene will be interpreted by your audience to have meaning regardless of whether or not it can be articulated.

To explore the relationship between time and the dynamics of a scene

Think back to what was going on inside your body when you performed this scene for the first time. Perhaps your muscles were somewhat relaxed, your breathing was controlled and paced, your movement was deliberate and direct, and endorphins were being released into your body. Now think back to the third time you were asked to complete this scene. This time your muscles were probably tight, your breathing was in short spurts, your movement was somewhat erratic and disorganized — your mind became cloudy instead of clear. Lactic acids, cortical, and adrenaline were released in your body. You probably also found that your inner monolog was one of concern or panic or apprehension. The whole dynamic of the scene had changed, and yet all we did was adjust the time element. The time element is another factor to layer into your work as an actor.

88. Origami

I hope you are feeling creative and artistic today. Take a plain sheet of paper, sit down somewhere comfortable, and make something out of your piece of paper. You might make it into an airplane, a swan, or maybe a flower. You are going to have to fold your sheet of paper in many different ways to make your object recognizable. Do not cut or tear the paper — as soon as you have made an object, I want you to unfold your piece of paper and start again. See how many different objects you can make in fifteen minutes. Your objects do not have to look like works of art, but they should be recognizable. This is a race against the clock and a test of your imagination and hand-eye coordination. Do not start this exercise until you have put yourself in a creative state. Don't prepare in advance, just be focused. Once you have completed this exercise, review your findings.

Now repeat this activity, this time working from a standing position. See if this enhances your imagination. Perhaps you are able to come up with new objects to make and perhaps your imagination is ignited. Once you are finished, compare and contrast your findings.

Variables:

Come up with your own.

Discussion:

What was the first object you made? Why do you think you made that one first?

Did you hit a stumbling block part way through this activity? How did you overcome this hurdle?

How did you get to explore your use of hand-eye coordination during this exercise?

Purpose:

To develop your motor skills

This exercise involves a lot of coordination between your hands and your eyes. As you are folding and forming different images with your hands, it is your eyes that will allow you to see what needs to be adjusted to make these objects appear believable and realistic. It is the coordination of these different senses that complements the results. In your acting, the more you are able to synchronize your skills, the more you are able to maximize the outcomes. Utilizing your motor skills means that you are working at enhancing the coordination of your body. An actor who is well coordinated will have a distinct advantage in that he will have a better understanding of his body. He will be better able to govern its movements in a purposeful fashion that complements the characters he is playing. You are simply folding a piece of paper, and yet you are developing acting skills that will stand you in good stead for the rest of your life.

Learning to work within a specific time frame

For this exercise you have been given a limited amount of time to complete your task. I have given you a time limit to remind you of the fact that many parts of the acting process will demand deadlines. The rehearsal process (if one is given) will be limited. Stanislavski sometimes took a number of years to rehearse a play with his actors, but this is a luxury that rarely exists in our industry. Many actors I work with tell me their agents want one hundred and twenty headshots on their desk within the next week. It is up to the actor to get on top of this task and meet the deadline. If you are talented but unreliable, you will not go far in the world of acting. If you are a student in high school or a university, then you may be involved in what are known as U.I.L. (University Interscholastic League) festivals. These festivals allow schools to perform in competitions that normally contain "one acts" (or plays cut to one act) that must be no more than forty minutes in length. I have seen excellent plays that went over the time limit by ten seconds and were disqualified. Time limits are a controversial idea in the creative arts, and yet they are a reality. They exist in television, film, and in an even bigger way in commercials. You do not have to agree with all aspects of your field, however you will do well to embrace them, enjoy them, and try to create a smoother and more beneficial journey.

Chapter 17

Prop Exploration

89. Mind Molding

For this exercise, take a chair, look at that chair, and then go sit in that chair. That was easy enough, wasn't it? Now do this exercise again, only this time imagine that the chair is your throne. When you sit in your chair you should do so with the authority of a king or queen and give your throne the respect that a chair of such importance deserves. Notice how differently you sat in your chair this time from the first time you sat down.

How about using a pen? Take a pen off your desk, pick it up, and roll it around in your fingers. Now put the pen back on the desk and imagine the pen belonged to your favorite grandma, who is now deceased. I also want you to go with the idea that this pen is the only item you have left to remind you of this special person. Take a moment before picking up the pen. When you do pick it up, remember it is not merely an object, but an item that belonged to a very special person in your life. Notice the difference in the way you pick up and hold your pen from the first occasion. When you take an object and make it your own we can call it endowment of an object.

Now endow a number of other objects of your choice. Some possibilities are a brush, a toy cat, a pencil, a photo, or an ashtray. You do not have to use real situations or people in your life; you can work with imaginary concepts. For instance, perhaps you could get into your car and endow it as a car that has broken down on you four times during the past year. Work with this exercise using different extremes: what if the pen belonged to a kid who used to bully you in school, how does that change the way you handle it? Don't choose only positive or heart-warming situations, but really run the gamut.

Variables:

Try this exercise with different sounds. Perhaps the sound of a bell could remind you of when you were in elementary school and it was time for recess.

Discussion:

How has your appreciation for objects changed?

How did each situation influence the way you handled an object? What did you learn from this?

What value do props have for the actor?
How can a prop become an extension of the actor?

Purpose:

To appreciate the value of props

In this exercise you are opened up to the idea that each prop has a value of unique standing. You realize that a pen is not just a pen and a chair is not just a chair. Whoever the object belonged to and whatever context it has been used in will totally change the way you handle it. Let's say you are in a movie and you are given a small, clear plastic tube that is filled with red dye. You are told that the tube contains a deadly poison that is so potent that if it gets out it will kill anyone within a two-hundred-mile radius. Of course, you know that it is just a plastic tube filled with red dye that couldn't hurt a fly. Unfortunately, so do most actors, and so does the audience. Think about the number of times you have watched a movie and seen the actor faced with a situation such as this and not believed for a single second that what they were holding had a real value to them in any way. They have failed to endow the object with real meaning. How many times have you watched movies where people are being shot at and they seem so calm, even playful in their manner? It's as if they have no belief that they will be killed. They know that their fellow actors are firing blanks in their direction, so there is really nothing to worry about. Unfortunately for us, this comes across in their acting — or lack of acting. From now on, you will have the ability to endow any object for any scene. Remember that belief must start with the actor if it is to permeate to the audience.

To utilize your own life experiences

In this activity you can utilize your own life experiences. I mentioned the ideas of a grandma or a bully at school as examples. You do not have to use your own experiences, but you are entitled to do so if you choose. Actors cannot avoid using some of their own experiences through their acting because as human beings we are a sum of all our experiences. A great deal of your resources will come from the world around you; that is why it is so important for an actor to live a full life and experience the world around her. As an actor you spend your time imitating and recreating other individuals and exploring human nature, so the world around you is your playground.

90. Prop Contradiction

For this exercise, find two props. One of these props should be somewhat menacing in nature (such as a rock), and the other prop should be more passive in nature (such as a piece of paper). Take your menacing prop and mime a short scene of how you could use it in a malicious fashion. An example would be to throw it at another individual as a weapon (mime this). Now come up with two opposing ways of using this rock that contradict its menacing nature. Perhaps you could mime putting the stone gently on someone's back as it would be used in a hot stone massage. Perhaps you could use the rock as a foot scrub to gently brush away dead skin cells in a soothing way.

Now take your passive prop and use it in a passive fashion. An example of this would be to write a letter. Now do the same thing you did before and come up with two opposing and contradictory ways to use your prop. Perhaps you could run your finger up and down the sides of it like it is the blade of a knife. You could slice it through thin air with a chopping action as if it is a weapon. You could also write a rather nasty letter so that as you write, it's as if you are burning through the paper. Notice that you have been asked to come up with contradictory actions and not just different ones. In the first part of the exercise I gave you an example of a violent weapon, which became a soothing and calming accessory. In the second example I gave you an accessory for writing that became a potential weapon. You can use two opposing items of your choice provided you can contradict them in this fashion. Once you have finished, review your findings.

Variables:

Take a phrase such as, "I love you" and say it in a way that says, "I can't stand being around you!" How many different ways can you say, "I love you"? In other words, change the subtext of what you are saying. Take some different phrases and make them contradictory in this manner.

Discussion:

Were you surprised at the contradictions you came up with?

In what way does this activity redefine an object's potential purpose?

Identify potential challenges with this activity.

Give some examples of why prop contradiction is important to the actor.

Purpose:

To appreciate the diversity of each individual prop

The reason that I want you to take an item and totally contradict its usage is so that you can see the potential diversity that each prop has to offer. A cup of coffee is not just a cup of coffee, but can be used as a weapon to momentarily blind your opponent if need be. A tree may be beautiful to look at but can also be used to save your life as you hide behind it, escaping the glare of the bright beams in the Nazi concentration camp. The way you look at a prop, handle a prop, and perceive a prop can totally change its purpose. This activity reminds you to have a deep appreciation for props because they can totally change the meaning of a scene. When talking about Stanislavski as a child, David Allen says, "He had been given a stick and told to mime putting it into a flame of a candle. Stanislavski decided to do it for real. Of course it started a real fire."[1] It is important to use your prop(s) in a way that is relevant to the performance, which may differ from that of your day-to-day life.

To unleash your imagination

If a piece of paper can be a weapon, then anything is possible. Your imagination is unleashed and can take you in any direction it chooses. A director is always looking to unleash an actor's imagination because when this happens, the potential for incredible breakthroughs is present. If we practice utilizing your imagination in activities such as this, then there is potential that this will become an automatic process. When you were a child and you learned how to ride a bike, you were probably not very good at it. As you practiced, you became better and better until it became automatic for you. If you practice and practice using your imagination, you will have one certifiably incredible imagination.

91. Propoholic

For this exercise, choose a film script or a monolog that you have already been working on. It needs to be something that you know and have performed or worked in some way before. Please do this before you read any further into this exercise.

---

[1] David Allen, *Stanislavski for Beginners* (New York: Writers and Readers Publishing, 1999), 2.

Welcome back! By now you should already have the chosen piece. Perform your piece one time. I do not mean sit down and read it; I mean get up and full out perform it. Now, go find five items from around your house. The only stipulation is that these are hand-held items. You might come back with a hairbrush, a post card, a cup of coffee, a running shoe, and a pencil. Your mission, if you choose to accept it, is to introduce these five props into your script. In some form or fashion, incorporate all five items. But don't just incorporate them; find a way to justify their presence within this scene. You can do this any way you want. Maybe you prefer to work in the props one at a time as you work the piece. By the time you have finished this exercise you should have a justified use for all five props in your scene. Please realize that I do not want you to go and choose an easier prop that you think would work better or be easier to incorporate. Find a way to incorporate whatever you have originally chosen. Likewise, please do not introduce one prop and then give up. You may think there is no way you can introduce all five props, but there is always a way. Notice how your piece has transformed from when you originally started.

Variables:

Look at your piece and choose five specific props that you think would go with the scene. You can also incorporate a greater number of props if you like.

Discussion:

What challenges did adding these props give you in the scene?

Were you able to work with these props in a way that was justified and realistic?

How did adding props change the feel of your scene?

What is the value of props for the actor?

Purpose:

To get used to working with props

In this exercise you are asked to work with a large number of props and justify their use. Let's say you are working on a hospital drama and are playing a doctor. You are holding a clipboard, and at one point you have to look at the charts on the clipboard in reference to the patient in front of you. You are about to tell the patient that she has cancer. At the same time you have to make sure that you hold the clipboard at a specific angle so that the camera can catch it. To tell a woman she is dying of cancer is a challenging scene for any actor. Let's say that you have done a lot of your foundation work and discoveries and the scene itself is very moving. The director is very happy with your performance. The only problem is you keep holding the clipboard at the wrong angle. Three takes turns into fifteen takes, and that wastes a lot of time and money. Get used to working with props in your hands. I want you to feel comfortable working with props.

To create challenges and spark the audience's interest

This is as much a note for the director as it is for the actor. Have you ever gone to a play and wondered why the actors were just standing around looking very fake and uncomfortable? If you looked more closely, you probably noticed there were no props in their hands. Actors generally enjoy props because it gives them something to do and something to focus on. As you go through your day, notice how many items you pick up or fiddle with in some fashion or other. We are constantly putting things in our hands, so when you get on-stage and everything is suddenly taken away, it feels false and fake. There are times when props are not needed or when they are a distraction. However, there are numerous times when using a prop can add to the scene. Audiences are, for the most part, very visual, and props can add flavor to a show in this way. Props also create challenges for the actor that can become more interesting for us to watch as an audience. In a number of TV soaps you will see that the actors rarely have props in their hands. This is because it becomes much easier in terms of continuity to take all the props away. Of course, it also looks fake and unrealistic for the audience and feels uncomfortable for the actor.

Chapter 18
Retention and Understanding

92. Room with a View

Choose a room in your house and spend one minute looking at everything you can see, making mental notes. Perhaps you can see a painting of a clown on the left wall and a cookbook on the dinner table. After approximately one minute, close your eyes. At this point, see how much you can recall of what you've just observed. Be very specific. Instead of saying there is a picture on the wall, say, "There is a picture of an old man with a blue shirt, a frown on his face, he is sitting in a field chewing a piece of straw, there are blue skies, and it is a sunny day. The picture is situated in the upper-left-hand corner as I am facing forward." You are going for as much detail as possible during this activity. If you would like, you can change the length of time you have to observe the objects in the room. You can also take a different track on how to recall the items you saw. Once your time is up you can go into another room and write down on a piece of paper everything you can remember. Again, the key to this activity is getting the detail and not simply broad descriptions.

Variables:

You can make this activity even more challenging if you so choose. Finish observing and then go into another room and complete some sort of mental task such as writing out your shopping list or doing a few difficult math problems. Whatever you choose, it should be some form of mental stimulation. What we are doing is creating a distraction to attempt to take your mind off the task at hand. Once you have completed your distraction, see what you can remember about what you saw in the room. You are probably going to find this a greater challenge now that we have put obstacles in your way. If you are in the wings, about to go on-stage for your scene and the stage manager starts talking to you, he has just caused a distraction. You will have no choice but to cope with that distraction, as you are about to go on for your next scene. The more you can prepare for such eventualities, the better.

Discussion:

Why is it important to memorize your lines with specific detail?

Why is it necessary for an actor to be flexible and ready for change at any given moment?

How could you work with this exercise in a totally different environment?

Why are the technical aspects of the actor's work so vitally important?

Purpose:

To improve memorization with specific attention to detail

Not only are you attempting to recall the objects around you, you are also attempting to recall as much detail as possible. While there are many benefits to the actor in having a good memory (such as line learning and recalling certain blocking for a scene), the detail portion of memorization is equally, if not more, important. Let's say you are reviewing your lines for a scene that is going to be filmed tomorrow. You find that you are very good at learning your lines in a general sense, but have a lot of trouble getting them completely correct. You know that you have had this trouble in the past, and as a result of your line fumbling, the same scene had to be shot an extra five times. When a writer completes her play, there is not one word that is a mistake or meant to be left out. In other words, it is your job as an actor to find a level of precision and accuracy. As Russ Weatherford points out so well in his book, *Confidence and Clarity,* "Lines solidly learned allow the actor to interpret the writer's words and the director's concept; thus freeing him to go into his most important creative achievement: make-believe."[1]

Learning to use your time efficiently

If you follow this activity as it is originally set out, you will only have one minute to recall correctly as many items as possible. This puts an added pressure on you in that you are going to have to work extremely fast. If you are in a movie and at the last minute the director comes to you with some new line edits, how are you going to react? Are you going to crumble under the pressure, or are you going to take the edits and get to work? The business you are in is an unpredictable one with many challenges along the way; you want to do everything you possibly can to make sure you are ready for those challenges.

---

[1]Russ Weatherford, John R. Weatherford, and Ruth Warrick, *Confidence and Clarity* (Hollywood, CA: The Weatherford Group, 1992), 6.

93. Rat Race

I call this activity "Rat Race," not because it involves acting with rats, but because rats serve as the premise of this activity. Walk down the street, observing things along the way. Walk for about two or three minutes, then try to remember what you just saw. The difference between this activity and other memorization exercises is that in this case I want you to remember everything you just saw in reverse order. In other words, I want you to remember the last thing you saw first. You might say, "The postbox, the blue Toyota Corolla, the white picket fence," etc. I know you are still wondering what this has to do with rats, so I will fill you in. Rats have an excellent sense of memory. They also have a fascinating technique of learning things by retracing their steps and the objects they pass along the way. Basically, I want you to retrace your steps in this activity just as if you were a rat.

Variables:

You can do this activity quite comfortably by walking around your garden and making observations of everything you see. You could also walk around your house and apartment and do the same thing. You don't have to have a time limit, but if one room is too easy, try going through two or three.

Discussion:

How effective did you find this as a memorization technique?
What are the complexities involved in remembering in reverse order?
Is this technique something you can use for other areas in your life?

Purpose:

To increase your cognitive learning skills

This activity is as much about widening your learning skills as it is about memorization. While you are being asked to memorize what you saw, you are also being given a different way in which to do this. As an actor, you are constantly being asked to introduce new learning skills and, in some cases, appear to be a master of them. You may find yourself being asked to play the role of a musician, a magician, a tailor, or a doctor. Each of these would require specific learning skills for you to emulate. As an actor, it is important that you are always willing to learn new skills even when it means learning something that is totally alien to you. The only certainty in the acting world is that there is no certainty.

To enhance your memorization capabilities

I cannot emphasize enough the importance of sharpening your memorization skills. I know you are aware that you use memorization for learning lines, but there are so many other factors to consider. When remembering or recreating your movement and positioning, you will utilize your imagination and memory. When doing research for a role, you will want to digest some of the information for later use. When auditioning, you will want to remember everything the director asks you to do on the first occasion (there might not be another). As a tool, memorization affects so much of what we do that the more ways an actor has to sharpen this skill, the better.

94. Light and Shade

Wait to do this exercise until you are completely alone. Go into a room that is completely dark. To achieve this you are probably going to have to do this exercise at night. Sit down in the middle of the room in complete darkness and silence. Please do not lie down on the bed for this exercise because you sleep on the bed at night and are used to the dark in that particular context. Stay there for the next twenty minutes. Make sure that your cell phone is turned off. If there are other phones in the house, you can leave them switched on, but please do not answer them during this exercise. As you are sitting there, notice what is going on for you mentally and physically. Do you feel any fear of being on your own? Do your muscles feel tighter than normal? Have you suddenly become aware of every little sound and creak in the house? Are you starting to think of all the scary things that have happened in your life or that you have heard about? Do you feel the adrenaline pumping through your body? Are you comfortable, or are you looking to end this activity as soon as possible? Make a mental note of everything that occurred for you during this time.

After the twenty minutes are up, take a couple of minutes to put your body back into balance. Stand up and shake everything out. When you feel balanced, sit down in the same room, only this time turn the light on. You are going to sit for another twenty minutes in exactly the same place. I would prefer that you use a ceiling light as opposed to a lamp so that the room is fairly bright. Make a mental note of everything you are feeling now. Do you feel more secure with the light on? Are you calmer and more relaxed than before? Where is your attention focused? How much attention are you paying to the noises and sounds around you? Make a note of everything that you are thinking and feeling with the light on. Compare and contrast your findings for both parts of this exercise.

Variables:

Work with different levels of light. You could work this activity using an office lamp. You could also put color gels over your light or use colored light bulbs and work the activity that way. Instead of using artificial light, you might want to work with daylight.

Discussion:

Was there any link for you between darkness and fear?

How can light or darkness cause such diverse reactions within us?

When sitting in darkness, did silence become more menacing for you?

If someone else was in the house, do you think you would have reacted in the same manner during this exercise?

Purpose:

To experience your reactions to light and shade

Sitting all alone in the dark may send a chill up your spine. This may be an automatic reaction that is out of your control. Five minutes ago you were fine, but now that you are sitting alone in the dark, panic starts to set in. Of course this may not have been your experience, but I am hypothesizing here. This is another piece of information you can use for your acting. If your character is walking down a secluded street in the middle of the day, she will most likely act very differently than if she were walking down that secluded street in the middle of the night. Sometimes it is easy to miss something such as the lighting or lack thereof because you are focusing on your character's motivations and justifications. As far as your acting goes, leave no stone unturned — that stone might be a vital step to creating truthfulness and honesty in your acting.

To understand and utilize self-memory

Let's assume you had been by yourself for most of the day and that you were having a really good time. You then decide to partake in this activity, and within five minutes you are sitting in your dark bedroom feeling very uncomfortable. How is this change possible in such a short period of time? Part of the answer lies in our past memories and associations. Perhaps two years ago you were sitting alone and you heard creepy noises that freaked you out. This past experience is triggered when you find yourself in the same position. You also associate darkness with crime and murder and danger because this is often the way it is portrayed on television and in the movies. You don't have to make these choices consciously because the mind and body have the ability to react automatically whether you like it or not. Pavlov's dog's conditioned response is a perfect example of this. Over many years, actors, somewhat controversially, have utilized self-memory. I am simply choosing to raise your awareness to its potential and the role it plays in your life.

Chapter 19
Research

95. One-Minute Play

This activity is exactly what it sounds like. Write a play that is one minute in length. There are certain ingredients that your play should have.

I would like your play to have a theme. By this I mean that you must decide whether it is a comedy, horror, "dramady," drama, action, or romance. Make a decision as to which genre your play is going to fit into.

Come up with a premise for your play. The premise is the overreaching arc of your story. An example of a premise is, "Love always ends in tears." If this is your premise, then everything you write should take this statement into consideration. Another possible premise is, "Good will always triumph over evil." Your premise is going to give you a clear direction to proceed with your story.

Develop a protagonist for your play. The protagonist is basically the hero of the story or the person to whom we relate. I would also like you to come up with an antagonist — the person who tries to stop the hero or lead from getting what he or she wants.

Bearing this in mind, make sure that there is some form of conflict in your play. Conflict does not have to be linked to violence in any way. Let's say a young girl was asked by her family to buy a loaf of bread and as she is skipping to the store the money falls out of her pocket and down the drain. She now has no money to buy the loaf of bread, thus a conflict has been established. Now raise the stakes. Let's say she goes back home and says she lost the money. If her mum tells her not to worry, then we really don't have a very convincing conflict. If before she left, her mother had said that if she did not come home with the loaf of bread she would be grounded for six months, we have created a high-stakes situation in which the girl would do everything possible to succeed.

Develop the denouement of your play. This is the turning point of your story whereby perhaps good overcomes evil and we can see hope for a brighter future. Perhaps it is the point where the two lovers have gone through their struggles and finally, with a passionate kiss, they realize that they are meant to be together.

Come up with a resolution for your play. The resolution is similar to the denouement but not quite the same. The resolution for the couple in love might be that we see them getting married. A resolution for the loaf of bread play might be that the mother realizes that the safety of her daughter is far more important than a lousy loaf of bread.

There are many other areas to consider, but for a play that is to be one minute in length, I think this is enough to be getting on with. Now, I am going to hold you to your honor that your play is between fifty-five seconds and one minute and five seconds in length. You are not allowed to go under or over these times. If you are having any time challenges, you are going to have to cut or add to your material. Once your play is complete and you are happy with your revisions, find some friends (actors) to act out the roles.

Variables:

You are more than welcome to choose to write a film script instead of a play. I would still like all of the aforementioned conditions met; however, you will also want to include many more notes to explain the action. If you have ever looked at a screenplay, you will realize that on a page full of scene descriptions there might only be two lines of actual dialog. If you choose to go this route, I would still like you to write one minute of actual performance in a movie that is one minute in length.

You could also try this project by writing a play with a different length such as three or five minutes. Whatever you choose, make sure you stick to the original length you set.

Discussion:

How did you come up with the premise for your play?

How did a one-minute time limit affect the way you wrote your story?

Did you feel that you had come up with a clear enough conflict for your story?

What was the biggest challenge for you in completing this project?

Purpose:

To appreciate different mediums within the acting profession

Let's say that your aim is to be an actor and that is all you have ever wanted to do. By having a greater understanding and appreciation for other fields such as writing, directing, cinematography, instructing, costuming, makeup, lighting, and producing, your acting will be more well-rounded.

In this exercise you are being asked to write a one-minute play.

While the length is very short, you still must include many of the ingredients that are involved in writing a play. The goal is that by the end of this project you will have begun to appreciate the art of writing a play or film (even if only in a small way). This may mean that the next time you pick up a script you pay more attention to the details. You might find that you immediately try to work out the premise of the play or who the protagonist is. While this in no way means you will choose to become a playwright, it does allow you to add a new element to your research and gives you a little more to appreciate or to criticize about the material before you. It would be exciting if you were able to experience some of the different elements that make up our profession. While I have heard it said on many occasions that no one man is a master of all, it is still useful to have at least the basic understanding of the different aspects of your profession. It is important to remember that acting is only one element of many that make a performance possible.

To work within a specific time frame

In this activity you are being asked to stick to a time frame very close to one minute. While one could argue that time factor is not an artistic element, it is a necessary one. If you are hired for a commercial that needs to be exactly fifteen seconds long, then you'd better be able to deliver your lines to fit this time frame. If the toothbrush needs to be able to be brushing your teeth on the third second and not the fourth, then you'd better be able to deliver the goods. Time is an element of the television and film industry regardless of whether or not we would like it to be. It is also a part of the theatre industry in a more subtle way. If a director can tell that a scene is dragging and taking way too much time, she is not going to let it slide. She is going to work the scene and guide the actors into finding motivations and justifications to keep the play alive. When a play is dragging, an audience can become lost, and it can be very hard to bring them back around. In fact, we could go on and on forever about the relevance of time in the acting world as it relates to auditioning, headshot mail-outs, networking, rehearsals, etc. The list is simply endless. This exercise makes you very aware of the fact that time is an enormous factor in your industry.

96. Interview

For this exercise you will need a pen and paper or a laptop. Interview three actors, directors, and/or instructors whom you admire.

They do not have to be famous people, just people you admire. Perhaps there is an actor at your college who you saw in a play and you really admired her performance. Perhaps your friend is an actor who does not book a lot of work but has an incredible attitude and believes in himself. Perhaps there is a director you admire whom you could ask for an interview. You may have an acting instructor you have worked with or who your friends tell you is excellent who might be well worth interviewing. I would like you to come up with a list of about ten questions. ("How long have you been acting?" "How much work do you put into character development?" etc.) You do not have to stick to the questions on your list. This is really a guideline that allows you to keep the interview moving in a timely manner. Be up front and tell them that you really admire their work and are looking to pick up some useful advice. It is very important that you find people whose work you admire and not just any three people. People love to feel that they are necessary and that what they have to say is important. There is no time limit for this exercise; however, if you tell them you only need twenty minutes of their time they may be more receptive to the interview. I want you to record what they are saying so that you are able to refer to their answers at a later date. If what they have to say is valuable you will want to keep it. It is not necessary to complete all the interviews on the same day; rather, you can complete them as the opportunities arise. Three interviews will give you a good contrast of opinions and will also give you the opportunity to look for similarities.

Variables:

You could interview people from all walks of life. This could be particularly beneficial for character study. You might interview the postman or the bank teller. Find out about their lives and their likes and dislikes.

Discussion:

What was your basis for choosing these people?

What was the most beneficial piece of information you got from each interview?

Did you find that your views differed from those of your interviewee?

How can you take the advice you got and use it in a practical sense?

Purpose:

To seek out good advice

This sounds like it should be a no-brainer, but sometimes it is not. Some actors will go round and round making the same mistakes again and again. While it is true you can learn a lot from your mistakes, there is a limit to how many you want to make. Getting advice from those you admire might save you a lot of time. You might pick up some information that takes out a lot of the guesswork for you. Another reason I want you to seek out good advice is because there is so much bad advice out there. Some people are simply out to get your money. These people are not necessarily going to give you the best advice. There are many books related to the field that can also guide you in your journey for a minimal cost. Do not take everything you are told as accurate. Listen carefully, take what you want, and disregard the rest.

To surround yourself with like-minded people

Your journey as an actor will be a challenging one, so it is imperative that you make it a little smoother by surrounding yourself with like-minded people. Let's say you have a friend who is an actor who is always negative, always complaining, thinks everything is unfair, and that acting really sucks! Even though he is your friend, you do not want to constantly be around this negative energy. What if you have fifty actor friends who think this way? Eventually it is likely to rub off on you and become very draining. I am not telling you with whom you should be friends, but try surrounding yourself with like-minded people who will encourage you and help you grow in your journey as an actor. When discussing the founding of The Group Theatre, David Garfield comments, "The future founders and leaders of the studio learned their craft, defined their theatrical ideals and ideology, and set out to revolutionize the American theatre and American acting."[1] A handful of the actors from The Group Theatre are Sanford Meisner, Clifford Odets, Stella Adler, Lee Strasberg, Harold Clurman, and Elia Kazan. All of these people worked together and grew off one another to formulate their own ideas. By surrounding yourself with like-minded people, you are giving yourself the maximum potential for growth and discovery.

---

[1]David Garfield, *The Actor's Studio* (New York: Macmillan Publishing Company, 1984), 1.

97. Movie Critique

For this exercise go and rent a movie that you have not already seen, but that catches your eye. Before you watch the movie, come up with at least five areas on which you can critique the movie. Some examples are the title, the acting, the cinematography, the storyline, the music, the costumes, the character development, the premise, and the originality of the storyline. To truly critique a movie you should write down the things you are enjoying and the things that you feel need to be improved. Instead of saying, "The acting stinks!" you might say, "I didn't believe the police officer because he had no feeling behind his lines." This is much more specific and explains your point clearly. A positive critique could be, "The setting in a beautiful dark forest really enhanced the movie and transported us to that place." Write your critique as you are watching the movie. Set up your different criteria before you begin and add new categories if you see something that you think is worth noting. Feel free to pause the movie if you are writing a comment and don't want to miss what is coming up. Please make your comments as specific as possible. It might require more than one sitting to complete the movie, and that is absolutely fine. If you love the movie and cannot find any faults, then you will end up with a very positive review. The word critique does not mean you have to criticize, rather that you have to find the truth according to your honest opinion.

Variables:

See Exercise 15: Movie Critic (page 34).

Discussion:

Do you think it is easier to critique a movie you enjoyed as opposed to one you detested? Explain your answer.

What was the biggest challenge in critiquing the movie?

On what basis did you select your criteria?

Is it necessary for an actor to be able to critique a movie in a specific fashion?

Purpose:

To highlight the different ingredients that make up a movie

In this activity you are made aware of the fact that there are many ingredients to making a picture. You get to explore in detail the many different facets of a movie that make it a great success or a terrific failure.

There are often two big problems in movies today, and both of them affect the actor. One problem occurs when the actor has a star complex and believes that only he is important. He does not realize that without the hard work of everyone including the producer, director, sound crew, light crew, makeup artists, and editor, the movie isn't going to be a success no matter how big a star he thinks he is. The other problem is that the movie industry seems to put less and less value on the role of the actor. This is somewhat understandable with the advancements in technology and special effects. The challenge is that if little thought is given to the acting in a movie, this will oftentimes lead to bad acting, and at best you will end up with a mediocre movie instead of a great piece of work. By doing your critique, you realize that each piece has to be just right for the movie to truly be a success in its entirety.

Although theatre has not been mentioned in this exercise, I would like to make a link at this point. David Mamet says, "I was fortunate to come up in the years when every performer entered show business through the stage."[2] There was a time when almost all film actors had training and background in the theatre. This is not the case anymore, and yet to ignore the theatre is, in my humble opinion, a catastrophe for the actor. How else will you get to work on a performance from beginning to end, to perform in front of a live audience, to sustain a role over a period of time, and so on? Most working actors look to film and television because this is where the money is. They are statistically right to do so if they want to make a living as an actor. But to never experience the theatre, to never perform in a theatre? As the influence of television and film grows and grows, an actor should never forget the roots of the craft that is and always will be performing in front of a live audience.

To develop your directing skills

In this exercise you get to see a film through the eyes of a director and decide what is working and what is not. You get to break down the entire movie instead of just the acting. Whilst a director certainly does not work alone, it is his overall vision that the movie takes. You may say you have no desire whatsoever to direct, and this is absolutely fine. It is still extremely beneficial to understand and appreciate the other aspects of your profession. The more well-rounded you are, the more appreciation you will have for what it truly takes for a project to become successful.

[2]David Mamet, *True and False* (New York: Vintage Books, 1997), 126.

98. Master Class

For this exercise go to the acting section of a bookstore or your local library and look at the different books on acting. Choose a book that looks to be of value to you and read it. Some possible authors are Constantin Stanislavski, Uta Hagen, Lee Strasberg, Stella Adler, Sanford Meisner, Antonin Artaud, and Jerzy Grotowski. Don't limit yourself to these authors; this list is merely a starting point.

Often, acting books will have practical exercises for you to do, so follow through with these. Make notes from each book on what is of value to you. If you have bought the book, then you can highlight the important points. I would always suggest browsing through a book before you purchase it so that you can see if it holds any interest. I would also suggest that you speak with your fellow actors about acting books they think are invaluable. If you trust their judgment, then this might be a good place to start. If you are a more seasoned actor and think you have read everything of value to do with acting, think again. There are a number of books out there that, although they are not directly linked to acting, do in fact have relevance to the work of the actor.

Once you have read one book and worked through it in its entirety, move on to another one. You do not have to agree with everything you read, but be careful not to make judgments until you have enough informed knowledge to do so. This does not mean you have to take everything for granted — just because it is written down does not make it right. My biggest note is that whatever you are reading, read with an open mind.

Variables:

Watch as many classic movies as you can. When I say "classic," I do not necessarily mean old movies. One good place to start is all of the movies that have won or been nominated for Oscars.

Discussion:

What is the most practical aspect of this activity?
Did you get any invaluable acting lessons for free?
Is this an exercise you can continue for the rest of your life?
Did any of these acting instructors feel like a mentor to you? Explain your answer.

Purpose:

To find a mentor near you

Let's assume for a minute that you have taken some acting courses in the area where you live and you didn't find them particularly beneficial. You have some experience in performing, but you still feel you would like to continue to grow and have a mentor to guide you. There are some excellent acting books out there that can guide you in the right direction and further your growth. I mentioned a number of authors whose books you can explore, and there are many others to consider also. It's a little bit like having these amazing people right in your living room with you, although not quite. Some actors/instructors will warn you against acting books because they say you can misinterpret what is being written. I would agree that this can happen, but even if you only get fifty percent of what is being said, that is fifty percent more than nothing. It is also sometimes hard to find an instructor who you see as a mentor who is looking out for your interests. You may find an acting book that gives you a whole new approach to your work. If you live in an area where there are few resources for the actor, then bring the resources to you.

To expand your knowledge in your field

The more you learn about acting, the less you will know. I know that this sounds like a contradiction, but what I mean is that as your knowledge base grows you will have more questions instead of less. You will be able to articulate questions that other actors cannot even comprehend. I do not mean this in a redundant, intellectual sense, but rather in a very hands-on and practical sense. It is a sad fact that some actors know nothing about their craft and have read nothing about it. I do not know any other field in which this takes place. The argument that I will receive is that research does not necessarily get you more work, and this is a valid argument. I still believe, however, that actors should be informed of their craft and its roots so that they are better versed and well-rounded.

99. The Business of Acting

For this exercise, consider some of the fundamental aspects of the business side of acting. Even if you are a student these are going to be important down the road so why not be aware of them now? A few points for you to consider:

1: How am I going to support myself?

You may say you will be a waiter or a bartender. These are possibilities, but these jobs are hard to come by. Do you have skills or can you get skills that will give you other flexible ways to bring in a good income?

2: Money.

Here it is again — that word with which you don't want to have to deal. Unfortunately, one of the main reasons actors leave the profession is because of lack of money. In point one we talked about jobs, but are you going to make enough money to support yourself? Are you going to have enough money to create a quality of life with which you are comfortable? I see so many actors who don't talk about acting as much as the stress of lack of money. Think this through and plan well because if you don't, it is going to come back and bite you on the ankles.

3: Can I stay in this for the long haul?

How long are you prepared to work at making it as an actor? Some actors say they will give it one year, three years, five years, and some say they will keep going their entire lives. If you are only willing to give it a year or two, then you are probably skating on thin ice. Statistically, many actors drop out after about three years. After three years they may have already done a lot of the ground work and built a solid foundation, and yet they drop out all the same. Look at point four and you will see part of the reason for this.

4: Have I set realistic goals for myself?

Let's be honest — there is nothing particularly realistic about telling your friends "I'm going off to be an actor," and yet if that is what you have to do then you have to do it. The question is: Are you willing to allow this journey to build over time? I hear actors tell me that within three years they are going to be a lead on a television show or movie. I like that confidence, but my concern is, what happens when they don't achieve their goals? Many of them leave and go back to their hometowns with shattered dreams. Setting realistic goals does not mean giving up on the bigger picture of your dreams, it just means you are prepared to get there in stages. Don't put yourself under so much pressure that you leave defeated with your tail between your legs. Set realistic goals that you can achieve and then build from there.

5: Am I prepared? Do I have a headshot, resumé, agent, manager, SAG, AFTRA, and Equity?

These are just a few things to get you started. By the way, there is an agent and then there is a better agent. I often hear actors complain about their agents, which may indicate it is time to build another partnership. There is also another piece worth considering. There is an old saying that goes "an agent takes ten percent and therefore you do ninety percent of the work." It is your job to go out there and find the auditions and get the work. An agent can submit you for auditions which you cannot submit yourself, but there is plenty that you can do yourself and be proactive. Just because you have a headshot does not mean it will sell your type or represent you. Does your resumé look professional? Do you have things on it that don't need to be there? Sometimes actors have not even attached their resumés to their headshot — do you think this makes a good first impression? Many actors want to join SAG and AFTRA at some point in their career, but these unions don't want you to join until you are prepared. Joining these unions is the beginning on your journey and not the end of it.

I have only given you a tiny and slimmed-down version of the business of acting. There are many other points that could be made, and I encourage you to do your own research. The reason I include this exercise in the book is because too many actors fail in their dreams because they have not even begun to consider this piece until they are right in the thick of it. The more prepared you can be, the more professional you can be.

Variables:

Research books on the business of acting. Look into seminars on the business of acting and try to find other people who have already taken those courses to get the thumbs up. There are a number of courses out there that are a waste of your time and money; do your research first.

Discussion:

Did you do enough research before rushing out to get your headshots?

Is it more important in the long run to have any agent or an agent with whom you can build a solid rapport?

Is your main goal to join the unions or to join the unions when you are ready to join?

How important do you think it is to have a good idea about how you are going to fund your dream?

Purpose:

To prepare you for the reality that awaits you

I am always concerned when I hear an actor say, "I went to an acting program and they never covered the business of acting." An actor who is trained to act but not to work is only getting half the picture. If you are looking to not only act but also to have a career in acting, then you have to be thoroughly aware of the business side of this industry. This is not just my personal belief, it is a fact. This exercise simply highlights a few areas you should be aware of and be on top of. Of course there are many, many more, but I want to get you thinking and planning in the right direction. It is very romantic to say, "I am tough and I can handle anything!" Maybe you can, but for how many years? Because there is such an enormous turnover in the field of acting, we know that this concept does not quite work. The more pieces of the puzzle you have already got in place, the smoother your journey will be. Things are already tough enough for you, so why pile any more onto the plate? Being a successful actor is going to take a successful team to support you, such as an agent, manager, photographer, and acting coach, to name a few. As Sarah Duncan comments, "When you are starting as an actor having an agent is a definite plus in the eyes of a future employer."[3] Preparation for the business side of acting is of fundamental importance if you are in it for the long haul.

To start to think about diversification

Some actors get very nervous when I say this. "I am going to only work as an actor and that's it!" If you can do this overnight, then I am very happy for you. Most actors, on the other hand, will need to use many resources to make their dreams into realities. What skills do you have that could complement your acting and also make money? If you were a massage therapist you would be developing your knowledge of anatomy and physiology, be making decent money, and have a flexible schedule for auditioning. I am not suggesting you become a massage therapist — it's only one idea. You could do work as an extra, work as an usher at a theatre, instruct acting for children and youth groups, instruct acting for adults, be a hairdresser, model, or work for an agent. I am not saying you must do one of these things, just that you must find ways you can keep yourself engaged in the field of acting while bringing in some income at the same time. There are always trade-offs. Decide

---

[3]Sarah Duncan, *Working Actor* (London: Cheverell Press, 1989), 38.

what you are willing to do for free to further your career and experience and what you are not. I understand that some actors feel that if they diversify they will not be focusing on their acting career. What I am saying is — unless you are very lucky — if you are not willing to diversify, you won't have any acting career.

Chapter 20
Auditions and Casting

100. Imperfect Perfection

This exercise may seem strange at first, and yet you will probably find it is something you are doing automatically all the time. Look in a mirror and critique yourself. For instance, you might say, "I have a big nose and it is ugly," "My hair is thinning and I look old," or "My teeth are crooked and goofy." Come up with a list of ten things that you can comment on purely based on physical appearance.

That was the easy part. Even though you may not constantly say these things out loud, you may be thinking them. What I would like you to do next is known as reframing. Take your statements and turn them around. They might now sound something like this, "I have a well defined and distinguished nose," "My hair is neat looking and sharp," and "My teeth give me a unique selling point in my appearance and help define my individuality."

Now this activity gets even trickier: Don't just say these statements, actually buy into them. It is easy to say things we don't mean but far more challenging to make these statements sincere and heartfelt.

Variables:

Instead of using your physical appearance, look at anything that needs reframing. Perhaps you could reframe, "I am too old," into, "My maturity allows me to utilize my experience and wisdom." "My other job is too tough," could become, "The job that allows me to continue in my pursuit and follow my dreams is character building." Start paying attention to the things you say and reframe them to your advantage. You can use this activity every day for the rest of your life.

Discussion:

What was the first thing about yourself you disliked?

How easy was it to come up with a list of ten observations?

What do you think about the concept of reframing?

What breakthroughs did you make when you were able to make your reframing heartfelt?

Purpose:

To enjoy your acting journey

As an actor, you are going to face enormous challenges along the way, and you want to make sure that one of those challenges is not yourself. If you are constantly putting yourself down, you are going to find that you're frequently depressed and angry. There are enough people out there who are only too happy to tell you that your feet are too big or your hair is too greasy; there is no need for you to be one of them. I am not saying that if your breath smells you should ignore it, but rather take action to solve the issue. If you are going bald, embrace it rather than fight it. You can either put all your energy into worrying about going bald or you can move forward and use that precious energy to focus on your acting career. Living in Hollywood, I see many actors who are not enjoying their journey. If you were to look at the turnover rate of actors out here, this would be very apparent. In this exercise you are asked to turn all of your self-perceived disadvantages into advantages. The smoother and more enjoyable the journey, the more likely that journey can grow and flourish.

To increase your chances at auditions

I bet this one got your attention. Think about it — let's say that you go to an audition and you feel that you are old. The casting agent asks you how old you are and you tell them in a way that is filled with negativity. Don't you think this is going to rub off? All your negativity will come out, and the audition will probably be over before it's begun. Now let's say you have reframed this experience earlier and you now see your age as an advantage that shows your experience and makes you a more reliable actress. Don't you think this will also come out in the audition? You want to sell yourself in every way possible, not only to those doing the casting, but also to yourself. If you think an audition is all about the performance, you are sadly mistaken. The audition begins as soon as you walk in the door, or, as one actor once told me in his case, as soon as he arrived in the parking lot. This activity will allow you to take whatever is holding you back and allow it to propel you forward. As Michael Shurtleff explains, "It's a total waste of your time to try to find out what the auditors want. What the auditors want is someone very interesting and talented in each role."[1] Allow them to see that in you by being prepared and through the positive energy you bring to each audition.

---

[1] Michael Shurtleff, *Audition* (New York: Bantam Books, 1978), 13.

101. Typecasting

This is an exercise that I have seen utilized in drama school and in an excellent acting book by Andrew Reilly called, *The Business of Acting*. Start off by coming up with a list of five or so questions. The idea behind these questions is to discover your "type." The questions can be as follows: How old do I look? What do you think I do for a living? etc. Once you have your questions, write them on note cards, buy a bag of candy and some pencils, and head to a crowded public place. You are going to ask people if they can take one or two minutes of their time to fill out the card with your questions. Now, you may want to use a little white lie. Tell them it is for a sociology project at college or something along these lines, and you may get a more willing audience. I mentioned buying a bag of candy because you may want to give a piece to each person who helps as a thank you. It is very important that you explain that you would like people's answers to be as honest as possible. It is of no benefit to you if they try to be kind and tell you that you look five years younger than you really do. You want their answers to be as brutally honest as they can make them. I would ask you to get at least fifty cards filled out so you can get a wide spectrum of people. Do not complete this activity at a school or college; I want you to get a real cross-section of ages. As stated in the title of this exercise, we are looking at your character type, and there is no better way to find this information than by talking with perfect strangers.

I know you are tired of hearing it, but safety first! I would suggest you take another friend or actor with you for this activity to keep you company or simply to make it more fun.

Variables:

Come up with your own.

Discussion:

Were you surprised by the answers you were given?

Do you see your type the same way as those who completed your survey?

Why do you think it is of absolute necessity that an actor know his type?

When an actor says he doesn't want to be typecast, why might this work against him in the acting world?

Purpose:

To know your type

This exercise is invaluable in that it allows you to find your type from those who know nothing about you. Their opinions are going to be about as unbiased as you can possibly find. It is imperative that an actor know his type because much of the acting industry will demand this. When you go out for an audition, if the role says "young, male surfer-type" and you are a sixty-five year-old man with a crew cut, this might not be the audition for you. Not only will you be wasting your time, you will be wasting the casting directors' time as well, and they will not take kindly to this.

I know that many actors want to be able to play any role and break the mold. I commend this and would say that the more work you command the more you will be in a position to do this. You will also hear of actors getting roles for parts that were written for someone quite different from them, or that roles were actually rewritten for them. These things do happen, but oftentimes actors are initially being seen for a role that fits their type and are then asked to read for something else.

If you are in high school or college, I do not feel this advice is as pertinent to you. This is one of the best opportunities for you to stretch yourself in different roles and even work on parts in which otherwise you probably would not be cast. I am not saying that you should be typecast by the industry, but unfortunately you will be, so take this information and use it to your advantage.

To book work as an actor

This exercise is about discovering your type in a very clear and distinct way. The aim is not only to help you understand your type according to others, but also to help you book jobs. There are many fine actors with excellent training who, when asked what type of roles they are most likely to be cast in, will say they don't know. The challenge is that they must know. Imagine getting sent on thirty auditions in a six-month period by your agent when you are only really the right type for two. You will probably get very despondent and feel that perhaps you are just a very bad actor. If you were sent on thirty auditions in which twenty-eight fit your type, you would have a much better chance of actually booking the work. In regard to the business of acting, Andrew

Reilly says, "When you go into business, any business, you must decide two things: what are you selling and to whom are you trying to sell it."[2] Many people call themselves professional actors but in their hearts feel conflicted because they are not being paid for their craft. The more pieces of the acting equation we can address, the more we can make this acting journey an enjoyable, meaningful, and more productive one for you.

102. Newspaper Ninja

Buy a newspaper that is current, flip it open to any page, choose the first article you see, and begin to cold read. Read the whole piece from start to finish without stopping. This is a cold read, so do this without reviewing the article in any way.

Now choose another article and spend two minutes reading through and reviewing it. Then do a reading of this article.

Take a short break and then turn to another article. In this reading, include all of the following elements: Make sure you do not look down at the page at all. The words you are saying do not have to be perfect. Look up so your eyes can be seen. Don't create a forced or fake smile. Stay yourself and stay unique. Do not slide your finger across the page, rather slide your thumb down the margin. Imagine the director is giving you instruction for the reading. Pay attention to what is being said before you begin. As you are reading, you should see the next few words ahead of you so you can plan ahead. For cold readings there are many other factors and this should get you started in the right direction.

You may have noticed that I have asked you to use a current newspaper for this exercise. This way you are able to use fresh material and also stay up-to-date on current events. The more an actor knows about what is going on in the world, the better. We are not in a position to go through life with blinders on, rather we must absorb as much as we can. This is an activity that I would like you to practice on a daily basis. If you do not have the time, work with it at the very least on a weekly basis. You need to keep your cold reading skills very sharp at all times.

Variables:

If you do not have time or the money to purchase newspapers on

[2]Andrew Reilly, *An Actor's Business* (Ft. Lauderdale, FL: Venture Press, 1996), 63.

213

an ongoing basis, you can use a book. I would prefer that you use a book that you are not too familiar with and randomly change the book you use. You can then continue with this activity in precisely the same way.

Discussion:

What newspaper did you choose? Why did you choose that particular newspaper?

Why is cold reading such an important part of the actor's tool box?

What are the many other factors that an actor needs to consider for a cold reading?

Purpose:

Audition preparation

This activity has you practice your cold reading skills in an incorrect manner without preparation and then proceed to add some very necessary elements. Your cold reading skills are very important in the audition process because you will often find you are given the script at the last moment. Although you may have five or ten minutes to prepare, this will still fit under the category of cold reading. You might feel that this is not as important to you if you audition mainly for theatre where you have to prepare a monolog. But what are you going to do if they suddenly ask you to work another scene from the play that you have had no time to prepare? Although a cold reading may have absolutely nothing to do with your acting ability, it often creates the first impression between you and the casting director. In fact, I would go as far as to say it is the only impression because if you fudge your way through the cold reading, you are not going to be asked for a callback. It is absolutely imperative that you not only rehearse your cold reading skills but also that you do so with all the necessary elements. I have given you a few things to consider; it's up to you to research the other elements that need to be explored. If you intend to become a working actor and stay that way, you are going to have to develop excellent cold reading skills.

To work on the technical aspects of your acting

In this activity you are working on your cold reading skills, which are a technical aspect of your acting. Unless you are involved in a reading of a play or voiceover work, you will hopefully never see a script in an actor's hands during a performance. Cold reading is a preliminary part of the actor's work; it also comes in handy if you are rehearsing scenes on script as you spend less time losing your place and slowing everyone down. However, the bottom line is that cold reading skills really have no place in the end product. If this is the case, why are they so necessary? If you do not have excellent cold reading skills, you may never get hired in the first place, and all your acting ability will go to waste. We cannot ignore the technical aspects involved in acting that go side-by-side with the artistic ones. Directors and casting agents are only human (well, sort of). If you make loads of errors in the cold reading, they are going to presume that you cannot act. This may be an absolutely false impression; nevertheless, it is an impression you have made. Don't allow any aspects of your acting journey to be left unexplored, no matter how irrelevant you consider them to be.

103. Casting Couch

For this exercise, sit in an audition waiting room and listen to everything that is being said by the other actors. For instance, one actor might be standing around complaining about how long it is taking to be called in. Another actor might be gossiping about the other actors in the audition. Pay attention to the secretary at the sign-in desk and observe her behavior. Observe the way that other actors are dressed and decide if they make an impression on you. See which actors seem self assured and together and which seem as if they are literally falling apart. Stay for a good while so that you can soak up the atmosphere and all that is happening.

Don't do these observations right before you are going in for an audition; rather, stay behind afterwards and do this. What would be even better would be to sit in on an audition you are not even trying out for. You can't do this just anywhere, but you'll be surprised by the number of auditions at which you can just sit in the waiting room without even being noticed.

Make notes while you are there and review your findings.

Variables:

See if you can create the opportunity to sit in on an audition panel as an observer. This is highly unlikely on a big budget project, but perhaps you have friends who are making an independent film who would let you sit in on their auditions. It would be invaluable to watch other actors at an audition. What would be even more powerful is to see the discussions that go on afterward about each actor and why they do or do not receive callbacks.

For another variable, see Exercise 104: Audition (page 217).

Discussion:

What was the most surprising discovery?

Did you see an actor badmouthing other actors or the audition? How do you think this behavior affected their audition chances?

Could you pick out those who were professionals and those who were amateurs?

Purpose:

To understand the audition process

Many actors believe that the only thing that counts during an audition is the try-out itself. In fact, nothing could be further form the truth. Let's say you arrive five minutes late to the audition, but it seems okay because they are running behind. You sign in and go outside for a cigarette because you are feeling nervous. The stage manager comes outside to tell you it is your turn to go in. You go in and know you have done a phenomenal audition. You go home pumped and await your callback. The panel indeed thinks you are excellent and unanimously agree that you should get a callback. The stage manager comes in and says no way. She goes on to explain that you turned up late and that she had to go outside and find you when it was your turn to go in. The panel trusts their stage manager and doesn't want actors that will be problematic, so you do not receive a callback. The only exception to this is if you are a superstar, in which case they will just replace the stage manager. By watching other people at an audition as an unbiased bystander, you will learn very quickly what to do and what not to do. The whole audition is a package, and what you do outside is just as important as what you do inside.

To know what auditors are looking for

If you ever get the opportunity to sit in at an audition, take it. Have you ever been to an audition and been told, "I liked your piece and I love your outfit"? You leave the audition feeling excited and knowing you are going to get a callback. When the callback never happens, you feel baffled. How could they give you such praise and not give you a callback? The reason they have told you these things is to get you out of the room in a graceful fashion. They want you to leave smoothly and quickly. Can you imagine if they told you that your audition really sucked? You would probably kick up a fuss and ask to do it again. What they say to you has little meaning and is really just lip service. It is only when you have gone out of the room and they start talking about you that the important conversation takes place. Unfortunately, you will not be there for that, so take everything they tell you with a grain of salt.

Never forget that it is *your* audition and that you should own it. If you are not quite ready, ask if you can take a moment. You will get your experience by going out and auditioning and also perhaps by taking workshops from well-respected instructors. How to find a good and reputable instructor is up to you. Do your research before you part with your hard-earned cash. As Michael Ray Lloyd explains, "We feel what actors need is a selective list of the top, professionally experienced, established and industry respected teachers and study facilities."[3] Remember that the next time someone tells you they love your outfit, it has nothing to do with you getting the part!

104. Audition

Act out the different steps of the audition process. You can do all of this in the comfort of your own home. You may use an audition you are about to go to or simply create a hypothetical one.

Let's assume that this is audition day and your audition is at twelve o'clock. Act out the process of your day. What time are you getting out of bed? Obviously you would want to wash, so why not follow through with this? Some people think it is a good idea to wear aftershave or perfume, but what if the casting agent/director is allergic to your perfume or finds it off-putting?

Act out getting dressed in what you are going to wear for your audition. If you are ironing now, I would question why you have not already prepared your outfit. If you have put time into thinking about your outfit, you should know exactly what you are going to wear and it should be ready before audition day. Some people don't put any time into what they are going to wear for an audition; then again, some people don't book work as actors.

What are you going to eat before your audition? Go into your kitchen and make some food. I suggest that you eat light. If you eat heavy foods, they are going to take a lot of time and energy to digest. You want to keep all of your energy for your audition. Avoid candy and sodas. These items contain high amounts of sugar, which are dehydrating. Make yourself a light and nutritious breakfast.

[3]Michael Ray Lloyd, *Hollywood Acting Coaches and Teachers Directory* (Hollywood, CA: Acting World Books, 2006), 1.

What are you going to take to your audition? Act out getting the things you need to take with you. Of course, this should have all been prepared the night before, as obviously a professional actor would not do this at the last minute. Are you taking a room-temperature bottle of water with you? I would — what if none is available when you get there and you develop a dry throat?

Are you going to rehearse your audition piece before you leave? Let's assume you have not received any sides/script and that you will not get these until you arrive. How can you possibly prepare when you don't know what to prepare for? You do know that the character you are playing is a business man/woman, so you can create a character background. Make some choices about who you are based on this limited information. You might say that this is pointless; why put all of this effort into an audition? Believe it or not, the auditors are not going to know that you are a fine actor/actress simply by reading your mind. They are not necessarily going to know this from your audition either, but the audition is all you have. If you don't get cast, you are not going to be able to show anybody anything. The audition process is of enormous importance to the actor even though it has very little to do with acting.

Why don't you act out arriving with plenty of time to spare at your audition? If you arrive late to your audition, do you think you have just made a good first impression? Arriving ahead of time is part of your job as an actor; if you cannot do this, don't be an actor — because you won't be an actor.

When you sign in, perhaps no sides are offered, so act out politely asking if sides/scripts are available.

Act out using this time to center yourself and focus on the audition itself. Act out finding your own space instead of gossiping with other actors with pointless and defocusing conversations.

Act out the audition itself. The key to this activity is not to sit on your couch and think about these things, but to get up and act them out in their entirety. Once you are finished, review your findings.

Variables:

See exercise 103: Casting Couch (page 215).

Discussion:

What does the food you eat have to do with auditioning?

What do I mean when I say you should prepare for your audition in its entirety?

Why is it important to go to each and every audition believing you will get the part?

Why is it important for you to understand the audition process in its entirety?

Purpose:

To prepare for the audition in its entirety

In this exercise you are being asked to go through the many steps of preparing for an audition. It is quite common for an actor to think the only important part of the audition is what happens in that room. Just as important are all the steps that get you to that room. For instance, if you eat a heavy meal before your audition, perhaps your energy level will be drained which will in turn hurt your potential for being cast. If you arrive late at your audition because of poor planning, you have made a very bad first impression. These people are human (although they don't always appear that way), and they will discuss these things. If you don't think this will affect your chances of getting the part, think again. Because this exercise asks you to get up and actually go through these steps, you get to see how much time, effort, and planning it takes to truly prepare for an audition.

To get the job

This exercise is all about getting the job because, after all, that is the only way anyone is going to see your work. You may not like the audition process, you may not agree with the audition process, and yet you have to go through the audition process. It never ceases to amaze me the number of actors that want to fight the system. Let's assume you are an amazingly talented actor and you believe that your talent will shine through whatever you do. Unfortunately, if you are not on the ball concerning all aspects of the audition, this is highly unlikely. You have a very limited amount of time, so you don't want to leave anything to chance. You want to put as many things in your favor as you possibly can. Let those at the audition define you so that you help them problem-solve. What I mean by this is that they need to find the right person for the right part, and if you fit the bill, you have just solved a problem for them. Some actors don't take the auditioning process seriously because they say it has nothing to do with acting and it is beneath them. These actors will unfortunately always struggle to get work even if they are tremendously talented. This book has been written not only to encourage you to continue to grow as an actor but also to help you actually work as an actor.

Chapter 21
Performance

105. Bio Mat

Note: Before you proceed with this exercise I would prefer that you have already completed exercise 101: Type Casting (page 211).

Find a new monolog to work with. You may say that you rarely use a monolog, but even if you are based in L.A. you may be asked to perform a monolog when auditioning for an agent. If you live in New York, your chances of needing a monolog are increased greatly. If you are a student, then a monolog will most likely be required for audition purposes. If for no other reason than to get up and work, everyone needs a monolog, so go find a monolog!

Actually, I am rather putting the horse before the cart, because I don't want you to find just any monolog, I want you to find one that will fit you perfectly. Find a monolog that is going to fit your type — a character that we could potentially see you getting cast for. While this might not be as relevant if you're an actor at school, it is still excellent practice for what lies ahead. You are going to research a piece that you feel fits your type.

Now, you may wish to choose a dramatic and heart-wrenching monolog, but for the purpose of this exercise, please don't. Realize that casting agents and directors are (almost) human and that after they have seen fifty depressing pieces in a row they are going to want to pull their hair out. I propose that you become a breath of fresh air. See if you can find a piece that is comedic at the start and has a surprising or heart-wrenching end. This will not be easy to find, and yet it will stretch your talent and hold your audience's attention.

Here is a big note that I would like to pass on to you as you select your monolog: Think of all those wonderful playwrights or screenwriters whose material you absolutely love. Think of your favorite film script that won an Oscar. You know exactly the scene you are going to work with, right? Throw that idea out the window (not the script). Understand that most directors and casting agents have seen these well-known pieces a thousand times and are absolutely fed up with watching them. Apart from that, they may already have preconceived ideas of how the piece should be interpreted. Find a piece that is not so well known. If you can find original, well-written material that fits your type, even better.

I also want you to find a piece that you can relate to and identify with in some way. We talked about type, so it is a given that it needs to fit your playing age. I realize that I am asking a lot, and it is reassuring to know that you are up for the challenge.

Once you have found your piece, learn it and explore it in a variety of ways. Once you feel it is ready for public viewing, take your piece to at least two separate laundry mats and perform for the audience there. This is going to take a lot of guts on your part, yet you could not get a more honest audience than the people at the laundry mat. Once you are finished, ask the people folding their laundry what they thought and whether they felt that the piece fit you. Be prepared for a variety of feedback and some very honest answers. (If you are young, please consult a parent or take one with you for this activity.)

If you try this out on a selection of your laundry mat connoisseurs and it doesn't fly, you may want to go back to the drawing board and come up with another piece. If, on the other hand, it goes down with a flurry of applause and accolades, you may be ready to try it out at auditions.

I wish I had come up with this idea myself, but I didn't. I was talking to a comedian who told me that when he is testing out new material he likes to go to the laundry mat. I simply took his idea and adapted it for the actor.

Variables:

Try taking your headshots to the laundry mat and get the honest opinions of the people there.

Discussion:

How long did it take you to pluck up the courage to actually go perform at the laundry mat?

What was the deciding factor in selecting the piece you chose?

What was the most profound comment you received at the laundry mat?

Acting is sometimes about courage. How does this apply specifically to this exercise?

Purpose:

To experience a real-world view

In this exercise you are asked to go out into the public arena and get a real-world view of your monolog. Sometimes actors get caught up in the world of acting. They get so caught up in it that they sometimes push reality aside. This exercise will bring you back down to earth in a hurry. You are going out and meeting real people who will share with you their real opinions. Sometimes actors claim that the only opinion they want is that of an "expert." I agree that this is very important, but so is the opinion of the paying public. It is not an "expert" who makes or breaks a movie but the paying public. They are the ones who decide what becomes a hit and what becomes a flop. If you are looking to go down into the annals of history, then it is your adoring public who is going to make this choice for you. You will also have a captive audience in the laundry mat because it is not as if they have anywhere else to go. Take advantage of this free performance space as the results could be invaluable.

To develop your confidence and courage

Be honest — when you saw that this exercise involved going to the laundry mat did you think about skipping to the next activity or simply avoiding the laundry mat part? Sometimes it takes guts and courage to be an actor, and not everyone is able to follow through in this way. There have been and will be many more times in your acting career when it is your courage that will see you through. Perhaps when you finish school and spend a couple of years acting in your local area you will decide to move to Los Angeles, London, Chicago, or New York. Provided you have enough money saved, a good idea of how you will support yourself with your day job, and the understanding that things will be very tough indeed, perhaps this will be a good choice for you. Nonetheless, it takes an enormous amount of courage and chutzpa to just get up and move. To leave a safe environment and move to the unknown is not something that everyone is capable of doing. There are going to be so many times in your acting career when your courage and tenacity will see you through. Any ethical opportunity that you have to develop your confidence is an opportunity you do not want to miss.

106. Sound Bites

For this activity, go through your music and find some songs that have no words. You may think that this is only the case with classical music, but — on the contrary — there are many CDs that will have an instrumental song of some sort. Another good place to find this type of music is a movie or musical soundtrack.

Pick three instrumental songs that you like. It would be beneficial if the three songs contrasted each other in some way. Play one of the songs three times. The first time you play the song, simply listen to it. The second time, think about what the song is about and what type of action could go with it. The third time, act out an improvisation to go with the song. Keep going, no matter what — really go with your gut feelings here. Allow the music to drive the action of your improvisation.

Once you are finished, repeat the exercise with the other two songs. At the end of this exercise, review your work. It will be interesting to see how each improvisation differed depending on the music you were working with.

Variables:
Come up with your own.

Discussion:
What is the importance of music in relation to acting?
What was the most profound lesson you gleaned from this activity?
On what basis did you choose those three particular songs?
If you did this activity again, what would you do differently?

Purpose
To set the theme for the play or movie
In this exercise, you get to tell the story that goes with the music. In a movie or play, this needs to happen the other way around — the music complements the action of the story. Think back to a time when you sat in the movie theatre and the opening song put you in a state of anticipation, fear, excitement, or even depression. A well-written score will be able to manipulate you in this way throughout a movie while keeping your focus firmly where it is supposed to be. If the music is randomly put together without real thought and consideration, it can throw off the entire production. This activity allows you to develop your appreciation for music as it relates to acting and the important role that music plays in enhancing many movies and plays. Each song tells its own story; the big question is, is it the right story?

To give you a kinesthetic sense of the importance of music
In this exercise you were asked to get up and act out the song as it came to you through the music. You had no choice but to feel where the music took you and allow your improvisation to develop. I could have said sit down and listen to the music and plan something out. This would have been beneficial, but you would not have experienced the results

firsthand. As an actor, it is important that you always maximize your learning and growing potential. At the beginning of this activity you were asked to simply listen to the music, and as you proceeded, you were asked to take it further and further. I am the first one to admit that I like to philosophize, analyze, theorize, and do all of that fun stuff. I am also the first to admit that there comes a time when you must put these ideas and concepts to practice in very real terms. This activity does just that by giving you a kinesthetic experience of what the music is actually saying.

107. X-tra

The title for this exercise is self explanatory. Consider experiencing being an extra on a movie set. If you are a SAG or AFTRA, member you will only be able to do union extra work. If you are non-union, there is still plenty of extra work for you to get involved in.

I know what you are thinking: "I want to be taken seriously — I'm not doing extra work!" If you are an actor who is constantly working, you can ignore this exercise. If, on the other hand, you are one of the many whose paid acting jobs are few and far between, you might consider extra work. I am not asking you to do it full time, just to get a taste of what it feels like to be on set. Perhaps this is something you could do once a week while you are building your career. See what it feels like to be on a set for twelve or fourteen hours. Some actors say that you should never do extra work because that is all you will ever get cast in. I would agree that there is no need to put it on a resumé or mention it at auditions, but otherwise you should be fine.

If you do decide to complete this exercise, you may be surprised at how much you pick up. While you are on set, talk to other actors and find out how their acting journeys are going. I would not recommend that you listen to all the advice you are given because it might be bad advice. It will be valuable to hear from other actors who have similar goals and dreams as yours. Why not experience as much as you can about your industry instead of sitting at home and waiting for the phone to ring? Having said this, be careful not to fall into the trap of getting comfortable in background work. This is not where your career should begin and end, but if you aren't careful, it just may. Take from this exercise everything you can and then move on. Some actors will use background work to get their SAG cards, but don't forget that you can also become SAG eligible in other ways. There is a method of allowing non-union actors to work on a union project provided that the actors eventually join the union as required by certain provisions of the Taft-Hartley Act. I am telling you this because while I want you to see the benefits of background work, I also want you to see the pitfalls. After a limited amount of time you should be ready to raise the bar and move on.

Variables:
Come up with your own.

Discussion:
Were you surprised at the number of hours you had to spend on set?

Did you get to watch an actor you admire at work? If so, what was the greatest lesson you learned from watching that actor work?

Did you pick up any technical concepts that you were not aware of before?

Purpose:
To get on set and learn
Acting is not theory, it is doing and experiencing. You can sit at home for the next five years waiting for your agent to call, or you can be proactive and do whatever it takes. Extra work can be beneath you when you can afford for it to be beneath you. While on set you might get to see some amazing actors at work. While many people may be sitting around bored, I want you to watch the actors whose work you admire and pick up as much as you can. It's like getting a free acting lesson every time you go on set. If you are there for twelve or fourteen hours, there is going to be an incredible amount to digest. Think of yourself as an absorbent sponge that is looking to soak everything up. Take a pencil and paper with you and make notes of anything and everything of value. You may be in a scene playing a nurse. You may have been told nothing about the scene that you are to be a part of except that you are putting away bandages. It is up to you to find out as much as you can about the scene by watching and listening in rehearsal. Gain as much information as you can so that you can bring your role alive. Even for a tiny role in background work you want to maximize your abilities as an actor and stretch yourself to the utmost degree.

To develop your stamina

It is not just extras who sit around on sets for hours. The stars often have to do the same thing. The only difference is that they have their own private quarters and you don't. Soap opera stars often talk of enduring grueling schedules that can stretch for many hours on an ongoing basis. If you add extra work to your repertoire, you will be used to all the hanging around on set, and by the time you become a big star it will be smooth sailing.

Stamina has another meaning in that you will need a great deal of stamina and staying power if you are going to have a career as an actor. No one is going to give it to you; rather, you are going to have to go out and make it happen. It is going to take stamina and perseverance to have a career as an actor. Many actors have wonderful ideas and beautiful dreams. What they don't have is the commitment, focus, staying power, and plan of action to make these dreams and ideas a reality.

108. Music Maker

For this exercise you are going to need a musical instrument. If you play an instrument, that will do nicely; if you do not, then you can grab something like a triangle or a tambourine or a bongo drum.

Find a song that you absolutely love and put it on your stereo. As the song plays, accompany it with your musical instrument. Become a very important part of the band, part of the ensemble. If you are playing the bongo, find the beat and play alongside. If you are playing a triangle, find the right moments to chime in and complement the song. Whatever instrument you are playing, put your heart and soul into engaging yourself in the music. The first time you accompany the music you might not be so hot, so I recommend you do this three or four times to get a really good feel for the song. The most important part of this activity is that you become part of the band instead of a separate force. It doesn't matter that you are not a musician; you will become one today. When you have finished, review your findings.

Variables:

Play many different songs on your stereo and become a band member with each one of them.

Discussion:

How exhilarating was it to be part of the band?

Did you get to a point where you actually felt like you were part of the band?

Were you surprised at how well you could accompany the music?

How does this stretch your belief in possibilities?

Purpose:

To become part of an ensemble

When you are playing along with the music, you start to feel like part of the band — maybe not the first time you play the song, but perhaps after two or three attempts. As a band member you now have a responsibility to keep in tempo/key with the rest of the band. In acting you have a responsibility to the other actors. It is your responsibility to know your lines, know your cues, know your blocking, and show up for all the rehearsals. It is your responsibility to be part of an ensemble. If you are working on a movie, the cameraman is part of your team, as are the lighting guy, the makeup artist, the wardrobe artist, and so on. Learn how to become a team member and to respect the roles of others on your team.

To build a kinesthetic response

In this exercise you are not only listening to the music, you are actually playing along with the music. You hit your drum along with the beat and the feeling reverberates throughout your body. You get a very physical sense and feeling of what you are doing. In your acting you could sit down and memorize your lines. You could learn them without even saying them out loud. You could sit on a couch and sort of rehearse a scene in your mind, but it is only by getting up and "doing" that you are able to put these things into your body. By physically rehearsing or performing a scene, you will get a real kinesthetic sense of what is happening. You will have the potential to make discoveries that you weren't even aware of. Acting involves action, so I suggest you get off your couch and act.

109. Off the Page

For this exercise, pick up any book that is not related to acting. Flip to any page and let your finger rest wherever it may. Then look at the next paragraph or the next six to eight lines of text. Read them and let them sink in because I am going to ask you to lift those words off the page and turn them into a performance piece. Learn your five or six lines. While you cannot change the words, you can change the context and setting in which they take place. Decide who you are. Where are you? What are you doing? What are the conditions you are already aware of? Develop a character background that is mainly going to have to be based on your imagination.

Let's say, for instance, that you picked up a book on gardening and it says something like, "As you dig into the mud you may find some parts are tougher than others. Make sure you turn the shovel really well and twist. If you get stuck, you are going to have to exert some extra effort so you can get deeper into the soil." If I took this out of context, I could say that this is a murderer telling his partner how to dig really deep to bury a body and hide the evidence.

When you take your paragraph out of context, you open up all kinds of possibilities. As I said, the end goal is to turn this into a performance using whatever tools you have. Once you are finished, review your findings.

Variables:

Work this exercise with a comic book.

Discussion:

Did you believe you would be able to turn your paragraph into a performance?

Can any words be turned into a performance?

What does it mean to lift the words off the page?

What was the most compelling breakthrough you made during the exercise?

Purpose:

To lift the words off any page

You have heard the term, "To lift the words off the page." This in itself is not new to you. What is more revealing is when you realize you can do this with any material. In other words, any text has the potential for dramatic action. No matter what the words or where you found them, they have the potential to be brought alive. This exercise has value to the actor in that it highlights your importance. You see that it is up to you to take these words and bring them to life. It is up to you to take the dialog and turn it into a performance that we remember. It is also worth noting that there is a fairly large amount of weak dialog nowadays. You may find this a lot with television scripts that are written and rewritten at a rapid rate. If this is the case, then it is still up to you to take those words and do something with them. Do not expect things to be handed to you on a plate because it just isn't going to happen. By taking any dialog and turning it into a performance, you are open to the idea that you can work with any dialog that is placed before you, no matter how weak. As an actor, you have to be a pragmatist. Instead of saying, "This is terrible!" learn how to take what you have been given and pull everything you can from it.

To understand the importance of the actor's role

In this exercise you are asked to flip any book to any page and bring it alive. This highlights for you the importance of your role as an actor. Without the actor we are left with beautiful — or not-so-beautiful — words on a page, and that is where they stay. If you venture out into the television and film world, be prepared. The role of the actor is being taken less and less seriously by these industries. This is certainly due in part to all the technical aspects that now encompass these arenas. Making a movie is such an enormous undertaking of logistics and manpower that the actor quite often gets left alone and is almost forgotten. While you might think this sounds great, think again. Without strong direction, the project can appear visionless and unresolved. It is up to you and the rest of the cast to do the work and make the discoveries, even if you have no strong direction. It is up to you to remember the vital importance of the role of the actor instead of falling into a lazy approach. On a film set most of those around you are not actors but crew members. They know and understand their craft and are very good at it. Getting the part is not the end of your journey, but merely the beginning of what you must accomplish. Do not look for support from those around you who are not trained in acting. It is up to you to bring the discipline and vision that acting requires to each and every project.

110. The Storyteller

See if you have an old copy of a children's book. If you don't have one, you can go to any thrift store and find one there. Read the entire story out loud as if you were reading to a group of children. Be sure to choose something that is fairly short in length — something that will take no more than fifteen or twenty minutes to complete. Don't just read the story out loud; rather, perform it and act out the characters as you go. Remember that you are supposedly reading for children, so bear this in mind in the way you utilize your voice. Children become bored very easily, so you are going to have to keep your reading rich and expressive. While you are acting this story out with children in mind, you should not make it superficial or unbelievable. Children are young, but they are not fools, so if you ham it up they are going to lose interest. Use the space fully, and don't be afraid to move around. Don't prepare in advance; the first time you read the story should be the first time you perform it. I want to remind you that you are reading this story as a performance, so there is no stopping if you make a mistake. Take risks and perform this piece full out. When you are finished, review your findings.

Variables:

Instead of working with a children's story, choose any story you like. Commit one hundred percent; if you choose a spy thriller, tell it in a way that gets this message across to the audience. Tell your story in a way that appeals to the sensibilities of its target audience.

Discussion:

How challenging was it performing a piece you had not been able to review ahead of time?

What are the specific challenges that come with telling a story aimed at children?

Were you sweating by the time you finished the story? If not, why not?

What does storytelling have to do with acting?

Purpose:

To become a storyteller

As an actor, you are a storyteller. You are constantly being asked to communicate a story to the audience. You can communicate verbally or non-verbally, and yet communicate you must. In this exercise you were given a children's story so that you could become aware of the expressiveness that is needed for this particular audience. To communicate a story to children takes an enormous amount of energy and commitment. As an actor it is not enough to kind of get the story across; it will require an enormous amount of commitment and energy on your part to get the story across clearly and succinctly. You may argue that you only have two lines in the whole movie you're working on, so this really does not apply to you. In truth, if your two lines are not communicated properly and with all the commitment and intent in place, something will always be lacking in that movie. You do not have to take my word for it. Think what happens when you are watching a wonderful movie and suddenly there is a scene that does not quite fit. I asked you to perform the complete story because as an actor I want you to get used to the idea of thinking of each project in its entirety and to have an understanding of the story from start to finish.

To work on and improve your sight-reading

In this exercise you are not given a chance to go away and learn your lines or even become familiar with the script. You are being asked to sight-read in a very raw sense. As if that is not enough, you are also being asked to perform this piece full of energy. You may think this is unfair, but get used to it. Sight-reading is going to be a big part of getting work in the movie industry. Let's say you are a very strong actor but your sight-reading is fairly weak. You figure that at the audition they will see through this to your incredible talent. I am here to tell you this is highly unlikely. If you cannot sight-read, they are going to say, "thank you," and move on to the next actor. Let's take this one step further and say you are excellent at sight-reading and always sound polished, yet you still book very few jobs and you can't figure out why. One comment casting directors say again and again is that actors don't know how to make strong choices in an audition situation. When you look at a script, you will see obvious choices that the scene will allow your character to make. This is the way ninety percent of those auditioning will play the scene. Look at these choices and then see if you can make different choices instead. Your choices still have to be justified and fit the scene, your sight-reading still has to be strong, but the idea is that you want to be remembered at an audition. If your choices stand out, then so will you. Even if you do not get the part, you won't go unnoticed. I agree with you wholeheartedly that sight-reading is not acting, and yet it is a part of the industry. This book is not just about exploring your acting, it is also about seeing you working as an actor.

Resources

The American Heritage Dictionary. New York: Houghton Mifflin Company, 1993.

Adler, Stella. *The Technique of Acting.* New York: Bantam Books, 1988.

Allen, David. *Stanislavski for Beginners.* New York: Writers and Readers Publishing, Inc, 1999.

Berry, Cicely. *Your Voice and How to Use It Successfully.* London: Harrap Limited, 1990.

Boleslavsky, Richard. *Acting.* New York: Theatre Arts Books, 1990.

Buscaglia, Leo. *Love.* New York: Ballantine Books, 1982.

Chopra, Deepak. *Journey into Healing.* New York: Crown Publishers, 1994.

————. *Quantum Healing.* New York: Bantam Books, 1990.

Duncan, Sarah. *Working Actor.* London: Cheverell Press, 1989.

Egri, Lajos. *The Art of Dramatic Writing.* New York: Simon and Schuster, 1946.

Erickson, Milton, Ernest L. Rossi, and Sheila I. Rossi. *Hypnotic Realities.* New York: Halstead Press, 1976.

Fast, Julias. *Body Language.* New York: Pocket Books, 1971.

Franke, Jessica. "Laughter: The Official Medicine of Captain Obvious." *Fibromyalgia Aware.* CA: Lynne Matallana, 2006.

Garfield, David. *The Actor's Studio.* New York: Macmillan Publishing Company, 1984.

Gilbert, Martin. *The Boys.* London: The Guernsey Press Co., 1996.

Grandstaff, Russell. *Acting and Directing.* Lincolnwood, IL: National Textbook Company, 1970.

Hagen, Uta. *Respect for Acting.* New York: Macmillan Publishing Company, 1973.

Harrop, John, and Sabin R. Epstein. *Acting with Style.* New York: Prentice Hall, 1990.

Hendricks, Gay. *The Art of Breathing and Centering.* Los Angles, CA: St. Martin's Press, 1989.

Hill, Napoleon. *Think and Grow Rich.* New York: Hawthorne Books, 1966.

Jennings, Sue. *Remedial Drama.* London: Pitman Publishing, 1973.

Johnson, Spencer, M.D., *Who Moved My Cheese?* New York: G. P. Putnam's Sons, 1998.

Jost, David. *The American College Dictionary.* New York: Houghton Mifflin Company, 1997.

Levy, Gavin. *112 Acting Games.* Colorado Springs, CO: Meriwether Publishing, 2005.

Lloyd, Michael Ray. *Hollywood Acting Coaches and Teachers Directory.* Hollywood, CA: Acting World Books, 2006.

Maltz, Maxwell. *The New Psycho Cybernetics.* New York: Prentice Hall, 2001.

Mamet, David. *True and False.* New York: Vintage Books, 1997.

Mobley, Jonnie Patricia. *NTC's Dictionary of Theatre and Drama Terms.* Lincolnwood, IL: National Textbook Company, 1995.

Morris, Eric. *Being and Doing.* Los Angeles, CA: Spelling Publications, 1981.

Reilly, Andrew. *An Actor's Business.* Ft. Lauderdale, FL: Venture Press, 1996.

Robbins, Anthony. *Giant Steps.* New York: Simon and Schuster, 1994.

Shakespeare, William. *The Complete Works of William Shakespeare.* London: Abbey Library, 1978.

————. *Macbeth.* Edited by Roma Gill. London: Oxford University Press, 1977.

Shurtleff, Michael. *Audition.* New York: Bantam Books, 1978.

Stanislavski, Constantin. *An Actor's Handbook.* New York: Theatre Art Books, 1994.

Weatherford, Russ, John R. Weatherford, and Ruth Warrick. *Confidence and Clarity.* Hollywood, CA: The Weatherford Group, 1992.

Wood, David, and Janet Grant. *Theatre for Children.* London: Faber and Faber Limited, 1997.

Yakim, Moni. *Creating a Character.* New York: Watson-Guptill Publications, 1990.

About the Author

Gavin Levy is co-founder of the Hollywood Stage Company with Paul Gleason at the Paul G. Gleason Theatre on Hollywood Boulevard. Their work focuses on the technique of acting and promoting the growth of working actors. Mr. Levy also instructs acting at the American National Academy in Studio City. In 2005, Mr. Levy saw the release of his first book, *112 Acting Games*, published by Meriwether Publishing.

Mr. Levy is a native Londoner who presently resides in Hollywood, California. He received his A.L.A.M. from the London Academy of Music and Dramatic Art, and he is a graduate of the Academy of Live and Recorded Arts, completing his training in 1995. After graduating, he continued his training through the Actors Centre in London. Mr. Levy has over seventeen years of experience in acting, instructing, directing, and writing.

While living in London, Mr. Levy became involved with the Impact Theatre Company and traveled to different parts of the country performing original works. As an active member of the Dragon Drama Theatre Company, Mr. Levy continued to work as an actor as well as coordinating and instructing acting workshops.

In 1999, Mr. Levy came to the United States to continue his acting and to further pursue his interest in the technique of acting for the professional and novice actor. Mr. Levy has written several plays including *A Day in the Life of Me and My Cup of Tea* and *Adam and Martha*. Both of these plays were produced at the Jefferson Playwriting Festival in 2000. In 2005, Mr. Levy participated in The Frontera Fest as both a playwright and a director. He is looking forward to more exciting and challenging projects in the near future.

Order Form

Meriwether Publishing Ltd.
PO Box 7710
Colorado Springs, CO 80933-7710
Phone: 800-937-5297 Fax: 719-594-9916
Website: www.meriwether.com

Please send me the following books:

_____ **Acting Games for Individual Performers** $17.95
#BK-B297
by Gavin Levy
A comprehensive workbook of 110 acting exercises

_____ **112 Acting Games #BK-B277** $17.95
by Gavin Levy
A comprehensive workbook of theatre games

_____ **Acting Games #BK-B168** $16.95
by Marsh Cassady
A textbook of theatre games and improvisations

_____ **Theatre Games for Young Performers** $16.95
#BK-B188
by Maria C. Novelly
Improvisations and exercises for developing acting skills

_____ **More Theatre Games for** $17.95
Young Performers #BK-B268
by Suzi Zimmerman
Improvisations and exercises for developing acting skills

_____ **Theatre Games and Beyond #BK-B217** $17.95
by Amiel Schotz
A creative approach for performers

_____ **Group Improvisation #BK-B259** $16.95
by Peter Gwinn with additional material by Charna Halpern
The manual of ensemble improv games

These and other fine Meriwether Publishing books are available at
your local bookstore or direct from the publisher. Prices subject to
change without notice. Check our website or call for current prices.

Name: _____ e-mail: _____

Organization name: _____

Address: _____

City: _____ State: _____

Zip: _____ Phone: _____

❏ **Check enclosed**

❏ **Visa / MasterCard / Discover #** _____

Signature: _____ *Expiration
date:* _____ / _____
(required for credit card orders)

Colorado residents: Please add 3% sales tax.
Shipping: Include $3.95 for the first book and 75¢ for each additional book ordered.

❏ *Please send me a copy of your complete catalog of books and plays.*

Order Form

Meriwether Publishing Ltd.
PO Box 7710
Colorado Springs, CO 80933-7710
Phone: 800-937-5297 Fax: 719-594-9916
Website: www.meriwether.com

Please send me the following books:

_____ **Acting Games for Individual Performers** $17.95
#BK-B297
by Gavin Levy
A comprehensive workbook of 110 acting exercises

_____ **112 Acting Games #BK-B277** $17.95
by Gavin Levy
A comprehensive workbook of theatre games

_____ **Acting Games #BK-B168** $16.95
by Marsh Cassady
A textbook of theatre games and improvisations

_____ **Theatre Games for Young Performers** $16.95
#BK-B188
by Maria C. Novelly
Improvisations and exercises for developing acting skills

_____ **More Theatre Games for** $17.95
Young Performers #BK-B268
by Suzi Zimmerman
Improvisations and exercises for developing acting skills

_____ **Theatre Games and Beyond #BK-B217** $17.95
by Amiel Schotz
A creative approach for performers

_____ **Group Improvisation #BK-B259** $16.95
by Peter Gwinn with additional material by Charna Halpern
The manual of ensemble improv games

These and other fine Meriwether Publishing books are available at your local bookstore or direct from the publisher. Prices subject to change without notice. Check our website or call for current prices.

Name: _____ e-mail: _____

Organization name: _____

Address: _____

City: _____ State: _____

Zip: _____ Phone: _____

❑ **Check enclosed**

❑ **Visa / MasterCard / Discover #** _____

Signature: _____ *Expiration date:* _____ / _____

(required for credit card orders)

Colorado residents: Please add 3% sales tax.
Shipping: Include $3.95 for the first book and 75¢ for each additional book ordered.

❑ *Please send me a copy of your complete catalog of books and plays.*

Order Form

Meriwether Publishing Ltd.
PO Box 7710
Colorado Springs, CO 80933-7710
Phone: 800-937-5297 Fax: 719-594-9916
Website: www.meriwether.com

Please send me the following books:

_____ **Acting Games for Individual Performers** **$17.95**
#BK-B297
by Gavin Levy
A comprehensive workbook of 110 acting exercises

_____ **112 Acting Games #BK-B277** **$17.95**
by Gavin Levy
A comprehensive workbook of theatre games

_____ **Acting Games #BK-B168** **$16.95**
by Marsh Cassady
A textbook of theatre games and improvisations

_____ **Theatre Games for Young Performers** **$16.95**
#BK-B188
by Maria C. Novelly
Improvisations and exercises for developing acting skills

_____ **More Theatre Games for** **$17.95**
Young Performers #BK-B268
by Suzi Zimmerman
Improvisations and exercises for developing acting skills

_____ **Theatre Games and Beyond #BK-B217** **$17.95**
by Amiel Schotz
A creative approach for performers

_____ **Group Improvisation #BK-B259** **$16.95**
by Peter Gwinn with additional material by Charna Halpern
The manual of ensemble improv games

These and other fine Meriwether Publishing books are available at
your local bookstore or direct from the publisher. Prices subject to
change without notice. Check our website or call for current prices.

Name: _____ e-mail: _____

Organization name: _____

Address: _____

City: _____ State: _____

Zip: _____ Phone: _____

❑ **Check enclosed**

❑ **Visa / MasterCard / Discover #** _____

Signature: _____ Expiration date: _____ / _____

(required for credit card orders)

Colorado residents: Please add 3% sales tax.
Shipping: Include $3.95 for the first book and 75¢ for each additional book ordered.

❑ *Please send me a copy of your complete catalog of books and plays.*